PSYCHIATRY - THEORY, APPLICATIONS AND TREATMENTS SERIES

OPTIMIZATION OF RESEARCH AND CLINICAL APPLICATIONS FOR COMBAT-RELATED POSTTRAUMATIC STRESS DISORDER (PTSD): PROGRESS THROUGH MODERN TRANSLATIONAL METHODOLOGIES

PSYCHIATRY–THEORY, APPLICATIONS, AND TREATMENTS SERIES

Attention Deficit Hyperactivity Disorder (ADHD)
Stuart M. Gordon and Aileen E. Mitchell (Editors)
2009. ISBN: 978-1-60741-581-7

Attention Deficit Hyperactivity Disorder (ADHD)
Stuart M. Gordon and Aileen E. Mitchell (Editors)
2009. ISBN: 978-1-60876-699-4 (E-book)

Victimhood, Vengefulness, and the Culture of Forgiveness
Ivan Urlić, Miriam Berger, and Avi Berman
2010. ISBN: 978-1-60876-191-3

Psychiatric Research Trends: Dreams and Geriatric Psychiatry
Daniella M. Montez (Editor)
2010. ISBN: 978-1-60741-760-6

Psychiatric Research Trends: Dreams and Geriatric Psychiatry
Daniella M. Montez (Editor)
2010. ISBN: 978-1-61668-719-9 (E-book)

Optimization of Research and Clinical Applications for Combat-related Posttraumatic Stress Disorder (PTSD): Progress Through Modern Translational Methodologies
Seth D. Norrholm, Tanja Jovanovic, Barbara O. Rothbaum, Michael Davis, Wendy Hasenkamp, Chris Crowe, Erica Duncan, Linda Leimbach, Kelly Skelton and Bekh Bradley
2010. ISBN: 978-1-61668-027-5

Optimization of Research and Clinical Applications for Combat-related Posttraumatic Stress Disorder (PTSD): Progress Through Modern Translational Methodologies
Seth D. Norrholm, Tanja Jovanovic, Barbara O. Rothbaum, Michael Davis, Wendy Hasenkamp, Chris Crowe, Erica Duncan, Linda Leimbach, Kelly Skelton and Bekh Bradley
2010. ISBN: 978-1-61668-358-0 (E-book)

War and Suicide
Leo Sher and Alexander Vilens (Editors)
2010. ISBN: 978-1-60741-978-5

War and Suicide
Leo Sher and Alexander Vilens (Editors)
2010. ISBN: 978-1-61668-274-3 (E-book)

Post-Traumatic Stress Disorder (PTSD): Causes, Symptoms and Treatment
Sylvia J. Egan (Editor)
2010. ISBN: 978-1-61668-526-3

Post-Traumatic Stress Disorder (PTSD): Causes, Symptoms and Treatment
Sylvia J. Egan (Editor)
2010. ISBN: 978-1-61668-716-8 (E-book)

Dyslexia and Depression: The Hidden Sorrow
Neil Alexander-Passe
2010. ISBN: 978-1-60876-118-0

Dyslexia and Depression: The Hidden Sorrow
Neil Alexander-Passe
2010. ISBN: 978-1-61668-933-9 (E-book)

Stress of Family Members in Caring for a Relative with Schizophrenia
Wai-Tong Chien
2010. ISBN: 978-1-60876-145-6

Military Psychiatry: New Developments
Dennis G. Stanton and Lawrence R. Castaneda (Editors)
2010. ISBN: 978-1-60876-149-4

"Paranoia of the Millionaire": Harry K. Thaw's 1907 Insanity Defense
Emil R. Pinta
2010. ISBN: 978-1-60876-988-9

Psychoanalytic Psychotherapy: A Modern Kleinian Approach
Robert Waska
2010. ISBN: 978-1-60876-909-4

Suicidal Behavior in Alcohol and Drug Abuse and Dependence
Leo Sher and Alexander Vilens (Editors)
2010. ISBN: 978-1-60876-919-3

Neurobiology of Post-Traumatic Stress Disorder
Leo Sher and Alexander Vilens (Editors)
2010. ISBN: 978-1-61668-851-6

Neurobiology of Post-Traumatic Stress Disorder
Leo Sher and Alexander Vilens (Editors)
2010. ISBN: 978-1-61668-816-5 (E-book)

Young, Violent, and Dangerous to Know
Michael Fitzgerald
2010. ISBN: 978-1-60876-952-0

Delusional Misidentification
Garry Young
2010. ISBN: 978-1-60876-956-8

Faranoia in the "Normal" Population
Antonio Preti and Matteo Cella
2010. ISBN: 978-1-60876-984-1

Malingering Versus Posttraumatic Stress Disorder
Kenneth R. Morel
2010. ISBN: 978-1-61668-144-9

Malingering Versus Posttraumatic Stress Disorder
Kenneth R. Morel
2010. ISBN: 978-1-61668-454-9 (E-book)

Cognitive Impairment in Children with ADHD
Alasdair Vance, Catherine Mollica and Paul Maruff
2010. ISBN: 978-1-61668-197-5

Cognitive Impairment in Children with ADHD
Alasdair Vance, Catherine Mollica and Paul Maruff
2010. ISBN: 978-1-61668-476-1 (E-book)

Immigration and Mental Health: Stress, Psychiatric Disorders and Suicidal Behavior Among Immigrants and Refugees
Leo Sher and Alexander Vilens (Editors)
2010. ISBN: 978-1-61668-503-4

PSYCHIATRY - THEORY, APPLICATIONS AND TREATMENTS SERIES

OPTIMIZATION OF RESEARCH AND CLINICAL APPLICATIONS FOR COMBAT-RELATED POSTTRAUMATIC STRESS DISORDER (PTSD): PROGRESS THROUGH MODERN TRANSLATIONAL METHODOLOGIES

SETH D. NORRHOLM, TANJA JOVANOVIC, BARBARA O. ROTHBAUM, MICHAEL DAVIS, WENDY HASENKAMP, CHRIS CROWE, ERICA DUNCAN, LINDA LEIMBACH, KELLY SKELTON AND BEKH BRADLEY

Nova Science Publishers, Inc.
New York

LIBRARY OF CONGRESS CATALOGING-IN-PUBLICATION DATA

Optimization of research and clinical applications for combat-related
posttraumatic stress disorder (PTSD) : progress through modern translational
methodologies / Seth D. Norrholm, Tanja Jovanovic, Barbara O. Rothbaum ...
[et al.].
p. ; cm.
Includes bibliographical references and index.
ISBN 978-1-61668-027-5 (softcover)
1. Post-traumatic stress disorder--Treatment. I. Norrholm, Seth D. II.
Jovanovic, Tanja. III. Rothbaum, Barbara Olasov.
[DNLM: 1. Combat Disorders. 2. Stress Disorders, Post-Traumatic. WM 184
O62 2010]
RC552.P67O68 2010
616.85'212--dc22

2010001171

Published by Nova Science Publishers, Inc. ✝ New York

CONTENTS

ABSTRACT

The state of ongoing military conflict in the Middle East and the recent rise in acts of domestic terrorism have created an increasing need for identifying potential vulnerability risk factors and for developing more effective treatment strategies for posttraumatic stress disorder (PTSD). Post-traumatic stress disorder (PTSD) appears to occur in a subset of vulnerable individuals after exposure to severe traumatic events. In order to tailor therapeutic interventions to the needs of the individual patient, it is important to develop a better understanding of the intrinsic and extrinsic factors that determine one's risk versus resilience for the development of PTSD following trauma exposure. The following chapter is a review of the most promising translational research findings that will help shape the direction and form for the optimal clinical applications for combat-related PTSD in the current military climate.

This chapter begins with a discussion of emerging findings from animal models as these basic science studies form the foundation upon which pre-clinical and clinical investigations are formed. Following this introductory section, we will highlight recent psychophysiological results that illustrate a direct link between basic science and clinical studies. Psychophysiological measures such as fear-potentiated startle and galvanic skin response have revealed several important findings with respect to the expression and inhibition of conditioned fear in humans. After discussing the translational bridge between animal models and clinical studies, we will discuss how these efforts have been expanded using virtual reality; a field that affords the integration of cutting edge technologies with established treatment and investigational protocols. Given the widespread administration of pharmacotherapies to individuals with combat-related PTSD, we next review the most promising pharmacological interventions to be used in conjunction with many of the established clinical approaches such as CBT and exposure therapy. Newly emerging pharmacotherapies will receive specific emphasis. Finally, evidence suggests that the differential risk for developing PTSD following trauma is due in part to genetically-mediated vulnerability and resilience. For this reason, we will close with a review of candidate genetic markers for risk versus resilience following exposure to trauma.

In conclusion, this chapter represents a comprehensive examination, intended for scientists and clinicians, of the state of translational studies of PTSD with special emphasis on the reciprocal process by which researchers and clinicians have "cross-fostered" their efforts toward the common goal of optimizing the identification and treatment of at risk combat-exposed veterans from the current military theaters of conflict.

Chapter 1

INTRODUCTION

The deployment of servicemen and women into the theaters of combat related to the Global War on Terror continues to produce mental health consequences such as posttraumatic stress disorder (PTSD), generalized anxiety disorder (GAD), and major depression [1]. At present, there are approximately 30 armed conflicts among more than 25 nations occurring worldwide [2]. Risk for developing mental health problems is directly linked to extended exposure to combat trauma, prolonged durations of deployment, and severe injury and/or disability [3]. As such, there is a compelling need to develop and optimize effective treatment strategies for PTSD and the related mental disorders with which it is often co-morbid. This chapter discusses the latest approaches to the treatment of combat-related PTSD with particular emphasis on what has been learned through translational research investigations.

Chapter 2

PTSD Diagnostic Criteria and Treatment Objectives

Posttraumatic stress disorder (PTSD) represents a constellation of psychological and physiological symptoms that result from exposure to a traumatic event that caused extreme fear, helplessness, or horror (criterion A). Symptoms are classified according to 3 clusters: re-experiencing (cluster B), avoidance/numbing (cluster C), and hyperarousal (cluster D) with diagnosis contingent upon duration of symptoms for at least one month [4]. As described by Ursano and colleagues (2004), the primary objectives for treatments that target PTSD symptomatology are: (1) the reduction of symptom severity, (2) the prevention and treatment of co-morbid disorders (e.g., major depression, substance abuse), (3) the amelioration of functional impairments, (4) the modification of dysfunctional fear learning processes, (5) the prevention of relapse, (6) the improvement of coping strategies for stress, and (7) the improvement of overall quality of life [5]. Ideally, symptom severity and treatment outcome are typically assessed through the administration of standardized, validated measures of PTSD such as the Clinician Administered PTSD Scale (CAPS; [6]) and Clinical Global Impressions scale (CGI-I;[7]). Not surprisingly, the heterogeneity of PTSD symptoms argues against the use of a single treatment strategy and for the use of a combination therapy to address the aforementioned objectives. A significant portion of this chapter will address how recent translational research findings may affect future clinical decisions regarding the optimal course of action for treating combat-related PTSD.

Chapter 3

From the Bench: Translational Research

There is a concerted effort among PTSD researchers to establish a reciprocal, translational bridge from the laboratory bench to the clinical bedside as a means of better understanding the etiology, progression, and treatment of PTSD (see Rothbaum & Davis, 2003; Ursano et al., 2009 [8, 9]). Translational research efforts in this area have traditionally involved the use of animal models to identify and study stress-induced neurobiological alterations that are phylogenetically conserved from rodents to humans [10]. For example, in rats, prolonged exposure to extreme stressors such as electric shock or restraint produces behaviors such as exaggerated startle and helplessness [11, 12]; behaviors that have been linked to the pathophysiology of PTSD and co-morbid major depression [4]. In addition, given the ability to manipulate genes in mouse models, bridging the gap between rodents and humans may lead to the discovery of novel genetic mechanisms that mediate PTSD and anxiety symptomatology. Further, translational methods may also uncover PTSD and anxiety-related "intermediate phenotypes," or psychobiological risk factors that are more proximal to underlying gene effects than parent disorders [13].

Translational Research: Fear Potentiation and Fear Inhibition

As part of the widespread search for intermediate phenotypes, rodent and non-human primate studies of fear conditioning have informed human investigations of fear learning and anxiety-related behaviors for the past two decades (for review see Foa et al., 1989; Miller and McEwen, 2006 [14, 15]). This is due in large part to the high degree of phylogenetic conservation that exists in both the overt fearful behaviors exhibited across species as well as the neurobiology underlying these behaviors. The acoustic startle reflex, for example, is a whole-body, rapid muscular response to sudden intense auditory stimuli that occurs in all mammals [16, 17]. The eyeblink component of the startle reflex has been consistently measured in human fear conditioning studies [18-22].

Fear-potentiated startle is defined as the relative increase in the amplitude of the startle reflex following presentation of a conditioned stimulus (CS; e.g., colored light) that was previously paired with an aversive unconditioned stimulus (US; e.g., airblast or shock). Fear-potentiated startle provides researchers with a powerful paradigm for translational studies of fear and anxiety, as it can be tested in animals and humans using very similar methods and it provides an objective measure of fear [23, 24].

The neural circuitry mediating fear-potentiated startle has been well established in animal studies and involves modulation of a brainstem circuit including neurons in the cochlear root, the nucleus reticularis pontis caudalis, and motoneurons in the facial motor nucleus and spinal cord [25-31]. The startle response is modulated by subcortical brain regions such as the amygdala and can be affected by the psychological state of the subject [29, 32]. For example, the startle response can be modulated by fear and anxiety-provoking manipulations [33].

Fear inhibition (and its putative impairment in PTSD patients) may represent an "intermediate phenotype" for the expression of anxiety-related disorders including PTSD. A paradigm for assessing fear inhibition in rats was recently translated to humans as a means of better understanding PTSD symptomatology. Myers and Davis (2004) developed a discrimination procedure in rats that allows for an independent evaluation of excitation and inhibition of fear.

The procedure, abbreviated AX+/BX-, is based on earlier learning theory experiments [34]. In this paradigm in rats, lights, tones, or air blowing from a quiet fan were used as cues A, B, and X. In humans, different colored squares were used for these cues. For example, a green square (A) presented with an orange square (X) was followed by an aversive airblast (AX+). On other trials, a purple square (B) paired with the orange square (X) signaled that no aversive stimulus would occur. As the subject learns that stimuli A and X presented together predict the aversive US (e.g. shock in rats; airblast in humans), stimulus A, the danger signal, becomes excitatory (ie., elicits an enhanced startle response). The presentation of stimuli B and X together predicts the absence of the US, and thus stimulus B, the safety signal, becomes inhibitory (ie., the startle response is reduced). The presentation of stimuli A and B together results in a reduced fear response compared to the subject's response to stimulus A alone [35]. The fear-inhibiting properties of B cancel out the fear-eliciting properties of A. Using this paradigm, Jovanovic and colleagues found that PTSD patients with severe symptoms displayed less inhibition on safety trials (BX-) and transfer test trials (AB) compared to healthy controls and PTSD patients with lower symptom levels [36].

This latter finding provides empirical evidence supporting the hypothesis that PTSD symptoms are related to an inability to inhibit fear in the presence of safety cues and provides a new avenue of clinical research in which impaired fear inhibition can be targeted in future pharmacological and cognitive therapeutic approaches.

Translational Research: Conditioned Fear Extinction

Cognitive and behavioral approaches to treating anxiety disorders typically involve exposure therapy, which consists of clinician-directed patient confrontation with fear-eliciting stimuli in a safe, therapeutic environment. These approaches are designed to foster fear inhibition. Through repeated exposure, patients can learn that a fearful stimulus no longer predicts a harmful outcome [37]. This form of treatment is based on Pavlovian extinction learning, or the process by which the association between a previously reinforced conditioned stimulus (e.g., an illuminated light; termed the CS+) and an aversive unconditioned stimulus (e.g., an electric shock; termed the US) is weakened through repeated, nonreinforced presentations of the US [38]. It is widely believed that the development of novel approaches for treating combat-related anxiety disorders will emerge from a better understanding of extinction learning and fear inhibition.

In order to discuss recent emerging findings in this area and their potential utility in clinical settings, it is first necessary to define the experimental terms and procedures typically examined in extinction studies. As described by Myers and Davis (2002), "extinction training" refers to the experimental procedure in which a previously reinforced CS is repeatedly presented in the absence of the aversive US. "Within-session extinction" refers to the quantitative reduction in a fear response as measured during extinction training, and "extinction retention" is the decrement in fear responding as measured at a time interval after extinction training. In clinical terms, exposure therapy, in which the patient is repeatedly exposed to fearful stimuli in the absence of harmful consequences, is the clinical homolog to extinction training [39]. In addition, the reduced fear levels displayed by a patient in a different temporal and spatial context following exposure therapy is the clinical homolog to extinction retention in the laboratory[39].

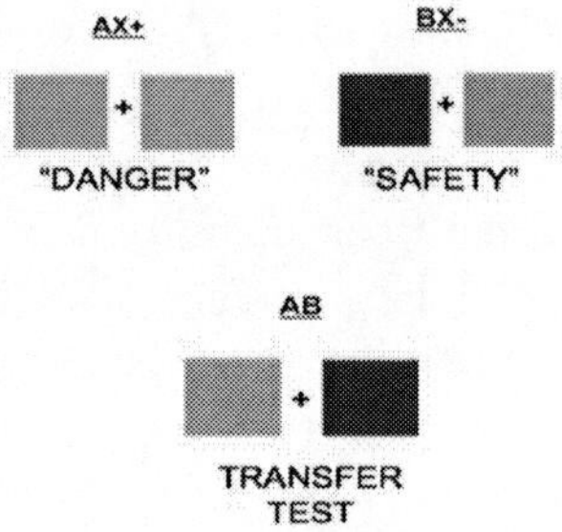

Figure 1. As part of the AX+/BX- conditional discrimination paradigm, stimuli A and X presented together predict the aversive US ("DANGER") whereas stimuli B and X presented together predict the absence of the US ("SAFETY"). The presentation of stimuli A and B together represents a transfer test such that fear-inhibiting properties of stimulus B cancel out the fear eliciting properties of stimulus A.

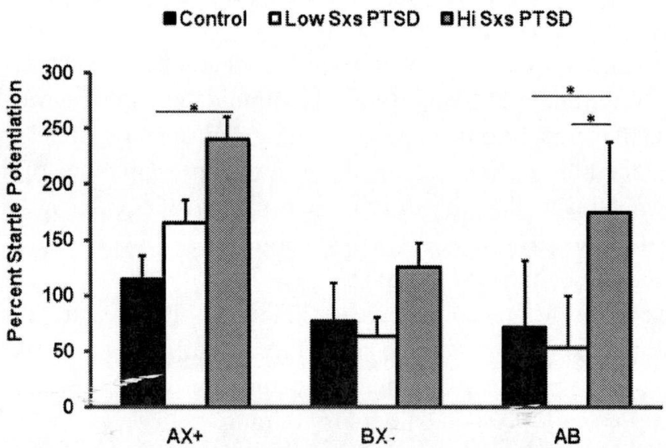

Figure 2. Vietnam veterans with severe PTSD symptoms fail to transfer learned safety in a conditional discrimination paradigm termed AX+/BX-. Sxs – symptoms; Percent Startle Potentiation = [(Startle Magnitude to Cue – Startle Magnitude to Noise Probe Alone)/Startle Magnitude to Noise Probe Alone] x 100. Adapted from Jovanovic et al., 2009.

Human studies of conditioned fear extinction have increased considerably in recent years. It has been postulated that some of the symptoms of PTSD may be the result of impaired fear extinction [8, 40]; a deficit that has been demonstrated in the laboratory using psychophysiological measures such as skin conductance, US-expectancy, subjective ratings of valence [41] and corrugator EMG activity [42]. Wessa and Flor (2007) used electroencephalogram (EEG), self-report measures, skin conductance, heart rate, and startle measures to show that the putative PTSD-related failure to extinguish fear occurs, at least in part, as a result of second order conditioning [43]. In other words, cues related to the original traumatic event (e.g., police sirens, smell of gasoline) become conditioned stimuli, elicit the unconditioned fear response, maintain fear by further reinforcing conditioned fear responses to new stimuli, and thus prevent extinction.

A fear-potentiated startle study of extinction in healthy volunteers demonstrated that individual differences exist in the rate at which recently acquired learned fear is extinguished [19]. It can be hypothesized that the ability to extinguish fear may be a *trait* marker for one's susceptibility to develop PTSD following a traumatic event. In a clinical application, individuals who display poor fear extinction using human fear extinction paradigms could be identified as at-risk prior to exposure to trauma (e.g., deployment to combat theaters) and treated accordingly whether through prophylactic means or soon after trauma. This idea is supported by work by Guthrie and Bryant (2006) in which firefighters were assessed before trauma exposure and then again after a traumatic event and the subsequent development of PTSD. In the latter study, deficient extinction learning predicted 31% of the variance in PTSD symptom severity.

Translational Research: Animal Models of PTSD

The development of novel treatments for PTSD as well as the search for potential vulnerability and resiliency factors for developing PTSD after trauma can benefit greatly from the generation of valid animal models of the disorder. To date, animal models of PTSD have employed methodologies such as predator stress [44], social defeat [45], the repeated administration of stressors such as shock and restraint [46], and prolonged unpredictable stress [47]. The paradigms listed above are each associated with the presentation of a stress or stressors that have been shown to elicit behavioral, neuroendocrine, immunological, and neurochemical alterations that are similar to the signs and symptoms linked to PTSD and anxiety [48].

There are several limitations to PTSD-related animal studies aside from the obvious species differences inherent with such an empirical approach. For example, the symptoms of PTSD often ebb and flow such that there are periods in which an individual reports or displays several symptoms from within each cluster at one time and other periods in which an individual is asymptomatic; animal models rarely account for this type of fluctuation in symptomatology. In addition, animal models typically do not consider the "dose" of trauma exposure that has been associated with the PTSD syndrome in humans. It is quite difficult to model the dose of a traumatic event related to combat compared to the dose of trauma associated with a vehicular accident. Similarly, PTSD, according to diagnostic criteria, can result from the perceived threat of death or injury or witnessing these perceived threats; these are also very "human" experiences that do not lend themselves to modeling.

The appeal of using animal models in translational studies of PTSD is that many of the neurobiological and behavioral abnormalities observed clinically can be produced using rodents and non-human primates. For example, repeated exposure to stressors such as shock and restraint during a short period of time can elicit anxiety-like behaviors such as exaggerated startle and learned helplessness in rats [9, 11, 12]; the latter behaviors represent features of PTSD and depression, respectively. Thus, the use of stress exposure animal models may inform preclinical and clinical studies aimed at developing treatment strategies for specific symptom clusters in PTSD and co-morbid depression rather than the global disorders themselves.

Chapter 4

AT THE "BEDSIDE": ADVANCEMENTS IN EXPOSURE THERAPY FOR PTSD

At the "Bedside": Exposure Therapy

Cognitive behavior therapy, which includes forms of exposure therapy, represents one of the most effective treatments for PTSD [49] and was the only therapeutic approach validated by the Institute of Medicine report [50]. The basis for many exposure therapies is the emotional processing model introduced by Foa and Kozak (1986). According to this model, the fear structure (which houses fearful memories of the traumatic event) must be activated and altered such that fear extinction and habituation can occur [51]. The desired end result of this process is the absence of conditioned fear responses, hyperarousal for example, in the presence of feared stimuli. Exposure therapy involves imaginal exposure in which the trauma is repeatedly relived in imagination in the therapist's office for 45-60 minutes. This recounting is tape-recorded and the patient is instructed to listen to the tape at home daily, practicing the imaginal exposure. Exposure therapy also includes *in vivo* exposure, or confronting the feared situation in a natural setting. One specific form of exposure therapy is prolonged exposure, or PE [52]. As will be discussed in greater detail below, virtual reality exposure therapy provides an immersive environment in which fear structures are activated in a controlled fashion within a therapeutic, safe environment.

At the "Bedside": Virtual Reality

Exposure therapy has been traditionally used as a first-line, non-pharmacological treatment approach for combat PTSD [50, 53-55]. However, its application has been somewhat limited in military populations which may, in part, be due to the perceived stigma within military peer groups and the military leadership hierarchy [1]. In addition, imaginal exposure therapy requires a high degree of emotional engagement in order to activate fear memories; this level of engagement is often absent or intentionally avoided following trauma exposure and in patients with PTSD [56]. Virtual reality (VR) represents an attractive alternative to "stigmatized" talk therapy and imaginal exposure therapy. VR can reliably evoke fearful memories through the use of immersive visual, tactile, and olfactory cues. It has proven effective for the treatment of PTSD in 9/11 World Trade Center survivors [57] as well as Vietnam Veterans [58]. Newly emerging studies have shown its validity [59] and success in treating combat veterans from Operation Iraqi Freedom (OIF) [60]. Reger and colleagues (2009) presented 93 returning OIF veterans without PTSD with virtual reality environments depicting an Iraqi cityscape as well as a desert convoy; two environments that are frequently encountered by soldiers deployed to Iraq [59]. Soldiers rated both environments as realistic representations of the actual scenarios into which they were deployed. This was a necessary first step in the dissemination and optimization of VR exposure therapies for treating cases of combat PTSD related to this theater of conflict. Full-scale clinical trials of VR exposure therapy are underway, yet early case reports have indicated positive results [60]. Figure 2 illustrates scenes from a virtual Iraq environment used by many clinical sites, including VA medical centers, for virtual reality based exposure therapy.

Figure 3. Screenshot images from a Virtual Iraq environment currently being used at several clinical sites for virtual reality based exposure therapy (from Virtually Better, Inc., Decatur, Georgia)

Chapter 5

AT THE "BEDSIDE": ADVANCEMENTS IN PHARMACOLOGICAL INTERVENTIONS FOR PTSD

In terms of pharmacotherapies for treating PTSD, the traditional approach has been to address the symptoms of the disorder with a combination of benzodiazepines or serotonin-selective reuptake inhibitors (SSRIs) and cognitive behavioral therapy. In fact, SSRIs (e.g., sertraline, paroxetine) are generally regarded as the first-line treatment for PTSD [61, 62]. However, consistently low response rates coupled with the lack of full remission in many patients illustrate the need for further exploration of pharmacological interventions for PTSD [63, 64]. In a very recent review, Berger and colleagues (2009) thoroughly examined the psychopharmacological approaches to treating PTSD over the past two decades. Drug classes, including antipsychotics, anticonvulsants, adrenergic-inhibitors, opioids, and benzodiazepines, were evaluated and rated according to the level of evidence supporting their therapeutic value for treating PTSD. Using U.S. Department of Health and Human Services Guidelines (1993), the Berger analysis categorized the drug classes as follows: (1) Level A – Multiple double-blind placebo-controlled trials with positive results (with level B criterion met), (2) Level B - at least one double-blind placebo-controlled trial with positive result (and level C criterion met), (3) Level C – anecdotal reports, case studies, and open trials with positive results and/or expert support, and (4) Level D - few case reports with positive results and no expert support [65].

In a manner that underscores the difficulty in pharmacologically treating PTSD with its associated symptom clusters, Berger and colleagues reported no instances in which a drug class met criteria for Level A of empirical support for use as a pharmacotherapy for PTSD. Of the remaining categorizations for empirical support, 5 of the drugs studied by the Berger group were listed at level B, 7 at Level C, and 13 at level D. The most promising agents, determined to be Level B by Berger and others, were risperidone and olanzapine (antipsychotics), valproic acid and lamotrigine (anticonvulsants), and prazosin (adrenergic inhibitor).

At the "Bedside": Antipsychotics

Risperidone

Results obtained from a small number of randomized clinical trials and open-label studies found risperidone to be effective in reducing PTSD symptoms when used as a monotherapy [66, 67] or as an adjunct treatment [68-71]. However, there were no reports of risperidone improving cluster C symptoms of avoidance or numbing [62]. In addition, one randomized clinical trial found no added benefit of using risperidone as an adjunct therapy (compared to placebo) [72]. Lastly, Rothbaum and colleagues (2008) reported that the co-administration of risperidone and sertraline improved insomnia symptoms as compared to placebo [73]. To summarize, risperidone appears to be a strong candidate drug as an adjunctive treatment for refractory PTSD in cases in which DSM-IV cluster C symptoms are minimal or absent.

At the "Bedside": Antipsychotics

Olanzapine

Evidence supporting the use of olanzapine as a pharmacotherapy for PTSD has come from a limited number of randomized controlled trials, open label studies, and case reports. The efficacy of olanzapine in treating PTSD symptoms remains inconclusive with some reports of decreased symptom severity after monotherapy [74] or adjunct treatment [64] and additional reports of no advantage over placebo [75]. A common benefit reported by at least 3 groups suggest olanzapine alleviates sleep disturbances and nightmares related to PTSD [64, 76, 77].

At the "Bedside": Anticonvulsants

Valproic Acid

Clinical studies evaluating the therapeutic value of valproic acid as a pharmacotherapy for PTSD have been favorable yet endorsement has been tempered by the lack of randomized controlled trials. In a randomized, placebo-controlled trial, Davis and colleagues (2008) found no significant advantage of valproic acid over placebo using four outcome measures for symptom severity [78]. However, valproic acid monotherapy was found to be effective in reducing PTSD symptoms in a randomized trial (without placebo control; [79]) and in open label studies [80-82]. In addition, patients reported significant symptom improvement when receiving valproic acid as an adjunct therapy [80, 82, 83].

Lamotrigine

With only one randomized controlled trial supporting its use as a pharmacological intervention for PTSD, there is simply not enough evidence to adequately evaluate the use of lamotrigine. In summary, the anticonvulsants valproic acid and lamotrigine show some promise as pharmacotherapies for PTSD, as determined by the 2009 Berger analysis, however, it is clear that newer drug treatments for PTSD will target a broader range of symptoms across DSM-IV clusters B through D and will address the underlying pathophysiology that mediates these symptoms.

At the "Bedside": Adrenergic Inhibitors

Prazosin

The clinical administration of prazosin as a drug treatment for PTSD symptoms has been based on the role of noradrenergic receptors in the neurobiology of anxiety-related behaviors [84] as well as the overconsolidation of fear memories that can occur with increased noradrenergic function [85, 86]. More specifically, alpha-1 adrenergic receptors have been implicated in PTSD-related sleep disturbances and hypervigilance [84]. Based on the findings of randomized clinical trials [84, 87, 88], open label studies [89-91], and case reports [92, 93], prazosin appears to be a reliable adjunct treatment for PTSD with specific benefits for ameliorating sleep disturbances and nightmares.

Based on the primary objectives for treating PTSD (according to Ursano et al., 2004), the 2009 Berger review was specifically focused on the reduction of symptom severity and the improvement of quality of life (objectives 1 and 7 from Ursano et al., 2004). The five drugs that achieved empirical support at Level B, according to Berger and colleagues, exhibited high therapeutic value for treating some symptom clusters while leaving other debilitating clusters unchanged. Recent translational studies suggest there may soon be a shift in priority toward treating the fear learning aspects of anxiety-related illnesses (objective 4 according to Ursano et al., 2004) as opposed to the symptom clusters that can arise from dysregulated fear processing [8]. As such, the most promising novel pharmacological treatments for PTSD may be those that have been found to enhance extinction learning in recent animal studies; most notably, drugs that alter neurotransmission in brain glutamate and gamma-aminobutyric acid (GABA) pathways.

From Bench to "Bedside:" Potential Pharmacotherapies for PTSD

At the Bench: D-cycloserine (DCS)

The potential use of D-cycloserine (DCS), a partial N-methyl-D-aspartate (NMDA) receptor agonist, as a treatment for PTSD arose as a result of numerous preclinical studies implicating NMDA glutamate receptor activity in learning and memory processes [94-97]. Antagonism of NMDA receptor activity has been shown to block both the acquisition of conditioned fear [98] as well as extinction retention [99-102]. Based on these observations, there was compelling interest to investigate the degree to which NMDA agonists (or partial agonists due to the potential for excitotoxicity associated with full NMDA agonism) could enhance extinction learning.

Researchers first administered DCS either systemically or directly into the amygdala of rats immediately before extinction training and then subsequently measured the degree of extinction retention 24 hours later [103]. Rats that underwent extinction training that received DCS displayed enhanced extinction retention compared to rats that received the drug without undergoing extinction training. These results demonstrated that DCS specifically enhanced fear extinction, as measured by fear-potentiated startle, and did not simply reduce fear responding. The enhancement of extinction by

DCS was later replicated by Rick Richardson's group in Australia using conditioned freezing as a measure of fear responses [104].

Based on these initial findings regarding DCS-enhancement of extinction, the Richardson group next analyzed the time course of this facilitation; more specifically, they sought to determine whether the observed effects reflected an enhancement of extinction consolidation. To accomplish this, rats were fear conditioned with a light (CS) and an electric shock (US) and then exposed to extinction training the next day. DCS was administered 30, 60, 120, or 240 min after extinction training. The authors found a time-dependent decrease in the enhancing effects of DCS as the interval after extinction training increased. The greatest degree of facilitation by DCS occurred less than 4 hours after extinction training suggesting that DCS acts to enhance the consolidation of extinction learning.

Molecular analyses performed by Yang and Lu (2005) have revealed some of the intracellular processes that appear to underlie the DCS extinction effect. For example, protein synthesis within the amygdala is required for DCS to facilitate extinction and the phosphoinositide-3 kinase (PI-3K) and mitogen-activated protein kinase (MAPK) second messenger cascades have been implicated in the DCS effect as well [105].

With regard to the behavioral extinction effects enhanced by DCS, further investigation by the Richardson research group revealed that DCS also appears to facilitate generalization of extinction [106]. Briefly, rats were fear conditioned to two separate CSs (a light and a tone) that were paired to an aversive loud noise (US). Twenty-four hours later, rats were exposed to two sessions of extinction training (consisting of six nonreinforced presentations of the light CS only) with the second session being immediately followed by an injection of DCS or saline. A second group of rats were administered DCS or saline without extinction training. Twenty-four hours after extinction training, rats were exposed to both the light and the tone without the US (test of extinction retention). Similar to previous findings [104], DCS-injected rats, compared to those injected with saline, displayed enhanced extinction to the light CS. Most surprisingly, the rats that underwent extinction training to the *light* that received DCS, showed a reduction of fear to the *tone* CS as well; an effect that was not seen in saline-injected rats that underwent extinction training to the light CS nor in DCS-injected rats that did not undergo extinction training. Thus, DCS administration produced a phenomenon similar to generalized extinction of fear in this paradigm, perhaps because of a great deal of context extinction. Because both the light and tone CSs were paired with the same aversive noise US, one explanation of this generalized extinction effect is that DCS enhances extinction by facilitating the devaluation of the aversive properties of the US. This finding is quite appealing to clinicians given that combat-related PTSD is often associated with more than one fear-eliciting stimulus [55].

As mentioned previously, an important aspect of fear learning of concern to clinicians is the return of fear following exposure therapy (extinction training). A large body of literature suggests that extinction does not represent an erasure of a fear memory but a form of new learning that competes with, or suppresses, the original fear memory [107]. Evidence against the erasure of the original fear memory comes from the observation that previously extinguished conditioned fear can re-appear with the passage of time (spontaneous recovery), a change in context from that in which extinction training occurred (renewal), or with the un-signaled presentation of the aversive US (reinstatement). In clinical terms, the latter phenomenon of reinstatement can occur as a form of relapse when a patient experiences a significant stressor following exposure therapy. DCS, in addition to its enhancement of extinction retention, has also been shown to reduce reinstatement of fear in rats [108]. In short, rats were fear conditioned to a light through pairing with footshock. Animals were then exposed to extinction training with one group of animals receiving DCS after extinction training while a second group was administered saline and an additional session of extinction training (to equate the terminal level of extinction in each group). A subset of these rats was re-exposed to the shock US by itself prior to a test session. Rats that received saline after extinction and an exposure to the shock US displayed a return of conditioned freezing through reinstatement. DCS-injected rats did not show the same reinstatement effect. From a clinical perspective, this finding is intriguing in that it suggests the possibility of pharmacologically inoculating against relapse in patients after exposure treatment.

At the "Bedside": D-cycloserine

Currently, several questions remain regarding the mechanism of action by which DCS facilitates conditioned fear extinction in rats and the generalizability of the aforementioned effects to human fear processing. In addition, there are a number of translational steps that need to occur before the potential utility of DCS as an adjunct treatment for PTSD can be fully evaluated. Previous reports have shown no benefit of chronic DCS as a monotherapy as compared to placebo for the treatment of PTSD-related numbing, avoidance, and anxiety [109]. However, some recent clinical studies have had promising results with the co-administration of DCS and exposure therapy.

Barbara Rothbaum and her collaborators at Emory University recently investigated the use of DCS in combination with virtual reality exposure (VRE) therapy for acrophobia, or the fear of heights [110]. It was hypothesized that DCS would enhance the therapeutic efficacy of VRE previously observed after a seven-week course of treatment [111]. Participants with diagnosed acrophobia were administered DCS or placebo 2-4 hours prior to two VRE "virtual elevator" sessions. Two dosage levels of DCS (50 mg and 500 mg) were used, however, there were no significant differences between the two drug groups and these data were later pooled. Only two sessions of VRE were administered as this was believed to be a suboptimal dose and would aid in reducing floor effects, and only two doses of study medication were administered prior to these two sessions. Assessment of treatment effects occurred at 1 and 12 weeks post treatment. At both post-treatment time points, those patients that received DCS in combination with VRE showed significantly reduced fear in the virtual elevator, as measured by skin conductance and symptom ratings, compared to those who received placebo and VRE. Similar to the effects reported by the Richardson group in rats, patients experienced a generalization of reduced fear of heights that extended beyond the virtual elevator context into "real world" contexts. Consistent with these findings, Hofmann and colleagues (2006) found that DCS co-administration with exposure therapy also reduced social phobia symptoms [112].

Preclinical and clinical studies have revealed some important caveats regarding the use of DCS as an adjunct treatment with exposure therapy; most notably, the dosing regimen appears to be a critical feature in this drug's capacity to facilitate extinction learning in rodents and patient learning in exposure therapy. Previous attempts at enhancing learning and memory through DCS administration in human populations have reported little or no effect (see Davis et al., 2006 [39]). The primary discrepancy, however, between the earlier human studies and the more recent findings reported by the Davis, Richardson, and Rothbaum groups is the timing of dosage. The former used chronic, daily administration whereas the latter studies employed single dosing before the learning event of interest. This point is clearly illustrated in a study by Quartermain and colleagues (1994) [113] and a recent study by the Richardson research group [114]. Both investigations showed enhancement of learning in animals with single, but not multiple, doses of DCS. Yet, a very recent study by Yamamoto and colleagues (2008) demonstrated an extinction enhancing effect of DCS in rats given the drug orally for 6 days following fear acquisition and during extinction training [115]. Thus, the timing of dosage and the route of administration will be important factors to weigh as emerging preclinical results are translated into future clinical applications.

Still at the "Bench": Cannabinoid Receptor (CB1) Agonists

Recent studies have identified CB1 cannabinoid receptors as a potential therapeutic target for drug treatment in humans based on the finding that CB1 agonist administration has been shown to facilitate extinction in rats and mice [116]. The latter effects appear to be due to an inhibitory effect on GABAergic/cholecystikinin interneurons in the amygdala that reduces the release of cholecystikinin [117]. As putative drugs acting on the CB1 receptor and cannabinoid reuptake processes are developed, this potential avenue of pharmacotherapy will be further explored.

Still at the "Bench": Valproic Acid (VPA)

Although it has been used extensively as a pharmacotherapy in military veteran populations for disorders other than PTSD, valproic acid (VPA; trade name: Depakote), represents a potential pharmacotherapy for anxiety disorders based on its newly discovered capacity to facilitate extinction learning in rodents and its activity as a histone deacetylase (HDAC) inhibitor.

Histones, comprise the basic protein of *chromatin* [118], the densely packed complex of nucleic acids and basic proteins that make up the chromosomes of eukaryotic cells [119]. Histone modification is a fundamental process underlying epigenetic gene regulation [120]. More specifically, histone acetylation initiates the early stages of chromatin remodeling so that DNA promoter regions are available for transcription factor binding and methylation [121]. These structural changes to chromatin underlie the regulation of learning-induced gene expression [120, 122, 123]. Reversing DNA methylation by an enzyme called histone deacetylase (HDAC) leads to less gene transcription. Inhibition of HDAC through agents such as trichostatin, sodium butyrate, or VPA has been shown to enhance long-term memory [120, 123-127] including conditioned fear extinction [122, 123].

The latter study by Bredy and colleagues (2007) identified histone modifications around individual brain-derived neurotrophic factor (BDNF) gene promoters as a mechanism by which the HDAC inhibitor VPA facilitates conditioned fear extinction. The expression of the BDNF protein and its gene transcripts, which are critical elements for learning-induced synaptic plasticity and long-term memory storage, are increased in response to fear acquisition and extinction [128-130]. BDNF has four transcripts that are regulated by specific promoters that are susceptible to epigenetic modification [121, 131]. The Bredy research group studied histone acetylation around two of these promoters in the prefrontal cortex of mice after fear conditioning and extinction.

Bredy and Barad (2008) very recently furthered their investigation of the effects of VPA on conditioned fear processing. The authors, using a white noise tone as a CS and mild footshock as a US, demonstrated that: (1) VPA facilitates both the acquisition and extinction of conditioned fear (as measured by freezing in mice), (2) VPA enhances extinction memory in the extinction training context and the original fear memory in the acquisition context (renewal), (3) VPA enhances reconsolidation of the original fear memory when mice were re-exposed to a single exposure of the tone CS, and (4) VPA can enhance long-term memory for extinction in more than one context if presentations of the CS during extinction training are sufficiently spaced in time. These findings demonstrate both the potential for using VPA as a novel therapeutic intervention for the treatment of fear-related mental disorders as well as the need to translate this work into the human clinical arena.

From Bench to "Bedside": Pharmacologic Summary

Traditional pharmacotherapies for PTSD have often treated the syndrome in its entirety with a specific emphasis on reducing anxiety-related symptoms. Recent translational studies of fear learning have suggested that a shift in focus occur within the clinical realm such that the future pharmacotherapies target the learning processes that underlie extinction-based exposure therapy. As seen in preclinical studies of DCS, there is the potential to enhance extinction learning during exposure sessions, to promote the long-term retention of what is learned during exposure, and to prevent relapse of symptoms following the cessation of exposure therapy.

Chapter 6

Risk versus Resilience for the Development of PTSD Following Trauma

In addition to a more focused approach targeting fear dysregulation, future pharmacologic intervention for PTSD may be governed by a shift toward personalized medicine. The identification of particular genotypes or gene expression patterns specific to trauma exposure and PTSD may dictate which drug treatments will be most effective for a particular patient. The long-term goal of pharmacogenetics was described recently by Ramey-Hartung and others (2008):

"Genotyping patients prior to beginning psychiatric pharmacological therapy can serve to inform practitioners as to each patient's likelihood of therapeutic response and their relative risk of experiencing toxicity and other adverse side effects from certain drugs. Such information could arm physicians with the knowledge they need to make appropriate drug and dosing decisions."

One aspect of pharmacogenetics, termed metabolic genotyping [132], looks at particular genetic variants in liver enzymes that may affect the bioavailability and efficacy of specific drugs. Of greatest interest to psychiatrists, however, is the identification of potential genetic variants that increase susceptibility for developing psychiatric illness and the subsequent effectiveness of therapeutic approaches.

An example of such a variant may exist in the gene that codes for the serotonin transporter (5-HTT); a trans-membrane, pre-synaptic protein that mediates the reuptake of serotonin from the synaptic cleft following transmitter release. A genetic polymorphism has been identified in humans containing a 44-base pair deletion in the promoter region (frequently termed the short or '*S*' allele) that reduces transcription of the gene, translation of the messenger RNA, and 5-HTT expression on the presynaptic membrane [133-136]. The 5-HTT '*S*' allele was recently linked to a predisposition for the development of PTSD following a traumatic event. For example, in a gene x environment study of Hurricane Katrina victims, those individuals who possessed the '*S*' allele and had low levels of social support were more likely to develop PTSD and major depression [137]. We will discuss potential genetic contributions to PTSD development in the aftermath of trauma in this section.

Potential Genetic Vulnerability Risk Factors

The treatment of combat-related anxiety disorders in military populations may benefit greatly from enhanced assessment of pre-deployment risk for developing PTSD following trauma exposure. It is increasingly likely that gene x environment interactions will be discovered that may identify at-risk individuals and subsequently allow pre-emptive measures to be taken prior to combat exposure. This notion is supported by recent findings from Segman and colleagues (2005) and Kilpatrick et al. (2007) in which particular genetic variants predicted both the risk of developing PTSD and the severity of PTSD symptoms. A review of the genetics of PTSD is beyond the scope of this chapter and there are several reviews currently available in the literature [138, 139]. Here, we will highlight the genetic variants and environmental interactions with the strongest empirical evidence and the greatest potential for impacting future therapeutic approaches to combat-related PTSD.

Epidemiological estimates suggest that greater than 75% of the general population will experience a traumatic event during their lifetime [140], yet as few as 5% of those exposed to a traumatic event will develop PTSD [141, 142]. Recent attempts to characterize individual vulnerability to PTSD from a genetic perspective have been impeded by several factors including, but not limited to, the complex nature of this disorder, the requisite exposure to a traumatic event that precipitates its development, the high degree of psychiatric co-morbidity with PTSD, and the litany of potential confounding factors associated with most genetic analyses.

The genetic background of PTSD has been examined through three primary types of investigation: family studies, twin studies, and candidate gene association studies. Each methodology possesses significant advantages and shortcomings. For example, it stands to reason that if there is a genetic component to PTSD, relatives of PTSD probands should be at an increased risk to develop the disorder following trauma exposure [13]. However, a limitation of family studies is that prevalence of PTSD within a family cannot be determined unless relatives themselves experience a traumatic event. Twin studies are beneficial for calculating heritability estimates yet do not allow for identifying the specific genes that are related to PTSD resilience, vulnerability, or chronicity. For the past decade, candidate gene studies have been the primary methodology for detecting genes that may influence development of psychiatric illness. However, the utility of candidate gene association studies for studying the genetic basis of PTSD has been diminished for two reasons. The first reason is inherent to all association studies: there is a low probability of identifying candidate genes that are specifically related to the psychiatric illness of interest [143]. The development of whole genome association studies, in which the complete genome of a patient is compared to that of a control subject, may lead to further developments in understanding the genetics of PTSD. The second reason is inherent to PTSD and its complexity: PTSD is a unique psychiatric diagnosis in that it involves an environmental etiologic event and its development and time course are undoubtedly affected by a combination of genetic and environmental factors [144].

Nevertheless, several major genotypes have been linked to either risk for developing, or resilience to, PTSD following trauma exposure (as reviewed by Broekman et al., 2007; [139]. Prior candidate gene association studies have identified genes related to the hypothalamic-pituitary-adrenal (HPA) axis, the ascending brainstem locus coeruleus noradrenergic system, and the limbic amygdalar frontal pathway that mediates fear processing [138, 145-147]. Within the latter anatomical systems, association studies have implicated the serotonin, dopamine, glucocorticoid receptor (GR), gamma-amino-butyric acid (GABA), apolipoprotein (APO), brain-derived neurotrophic factor (BDNF), and neuropeptide Y (NPY) systems in the genetic contribution to the onset of PTSD symptoms following a traumatic event.

Twin Studies

In the early part of this decade, much of the work investigating a genetic basis for PTSD was performed via twin studies. Examination of 3000-4000 twin pairs from the Vietnam Twin Registry revealed that approximately 32-35% of the variance of PTSD symptoms could be attributed to inherited influences upon exposure to combat [148, 149]. Consistent with these two twin studies of PTSD, Stein and others (2002) found that, when comparing twin pairs in which each twin experienced a traumatic event, identical twins were significantly more likely to be matched on post-traumatic stress disorder symptoms than fraternal twins [150]. The authors calculated that 30% of the variance in responses to trauma could be attributed to heredity. The authors of the latter twin study also found a genetic influence on the likelihood of falling victim to an assault. More specifically, identical twins, as compared to fraternal twins, were more highly matched for experiencing an assault and subsequently developing PTSD after the assault. As discussed by the authors, this may be related to the common genetic influence on temperament, anger, and irritability in identical twin pairs and the contribution of these characteristics to one's chance of being assaulted [150].

An ongoing concern for researchers investigating the underlying neurobiology of PTSD is the extent to which the biological markers identified in patients represent a *consequence* of the traumatic exposure and resultant PTSD or a *vulnerability* factor that increases one's likelihood of developing the disorder following exposure to trauma. Gilbertson and colleagues (2002) measured the hippocampal volume of Vietnam veterans with PTSD and their *unaffected* twins who did not enter the theater of combat in Vietnam. Both the cohort of Vietnam veterans with PTSD and their unaffected, non-combat exposed twins displayed smaller hippocampal volume compared to twin pairs that included Vietnam veterans without PTSD and their unaffected siblings [151]. Based on this finding, reduced hippocampal volume appeared to be a risk factor for developing PTSD following a traumatic event. Kasai et al. (2008) recently employed an impressively designed twin study of brain morphometrics and PTSD. In the latter study, two classifications of twin pairs were used. One classification included sets of twins in which one twin was combat-exposed in Vietnam and diagnosed with PTSD while his co-twin was unexposed to combat and did not have PTSD (co-twin was termed "high risk"). The second classification included sets of twins in which one twin was combat-exposed in Vietnam and did *not* have PTSD while his co-twin was not exposed to combat and did not have PTSD (co-twin termed "low risk"). Combat-exposed twins with PTSD had less gray matter volume in the hippocampus, pregenual anterior cingulate cortex, and bilateral insular regions compared to combat-exposed twins without PTSD. In addition, a Diagnosis by Exposure interaction revealed less gray matter volume in the pregenual anterior cingulate cortex of combat-exposed PTSD twins compared to the other three twin groups [152]. This very recent finding suggests that lower gray matter volume is a consequence of combat stress exposure and subsequent PTSD. Further studies should strive to include patient populations and control groups similar to those employed by Kasai and colleagues in order to better understand neurological vulnerability factors to PTSD as well as the consequences of trauma exposure. This will be especially important in the study of recently returning Iraq and Afghanistan combat veterans in order to assess the role of temporal proximity to trauma in the aforementioned PTSD-related morphological alterations.

Commonly Reported Genetic Variants

There have been several recent reviews on the genetic bases of PTSD (see Koenen et al., 2007; Broekman et al., 2007 [138, 139]). Thus, we will limit our discussion to the latest findings regarding the most promising genetic variants as well as potential GxE interactions that have been recently identified and warrant further investigation.

Serotonin (5-HT) Transporter (SERT)

Dysregulation of brain serotonergic systems has been implicated in the pathophysiology of PTSD [153, 154]. The basis for a serotonergic role in PTSD arises from previous work showing that: (1) 5-HT regulates sleep patterns, arousal, and mood [155], (2) antidepressants that alter serotonin activity effectively treat PTSD [153, 156], and (3) the psychiatric disorders with which PTSD tends to cluster (e.g., major depressive disorder) have been associated with serotonergic dysfunction [153, 157]. Recent studies have suggested that serotonin transporter (SERT) genetic polymorphisms contribute to an individual's response to a traumatic event [158, 159]. The serotonin transporter (SERT) gene, mapped to chromosome 17q11.1-q12, contains a polymorphism (*5HTTLPR*) within the promoter region such that there is a long *L* allele and a short *S* allele [133]. SERT expression at the pre-synaptic membrane and 5-HT uptake activity is significantly greater in carriers of the long allele as compared to carriers of the short allele [133, 134].

A study of Korean PTSD patients revealed a higher frequency of individuals with the homozygous *S* SERT genotype compared to normal controls [159]. Kilpatrick and colleagues (2007) reported similar results in a genetic analysis of trauma-exposed individuals who experienced the 2004 hurricanes in south Florida [137]. The authors of the latter study classified hurricane-exposed PTSD patients according to the degree of social support made available following trauma exposure. The homozygous *S* genotype was associated with a diagnosis of PTSD only in those who experienced high hurricane exposure and a low degree of social support.

The increasingly prevalent finding of an interaction between the 5-HTTLPR polymorphism and stressful life events as a vulnerability factor to depressive illnesses (e.g., Caspi et al., 2003 [158]) has spurred further explorations of this interaction to other psychiatric illnesses. Stein and others (2008) investigated the relationship between the 5-HTTLPR polymorphism, childhood maltreatment, and anxiety sensitivity [160]. Anxiety sensitivity (AS) has been defined as the fear of anxiety-related symptoms such that an individual fears his/her symptoms will lead to an adverse event (e.g., cardiac arrest; [161]). Scores on the Anxiety Sensitivity Index were previously correlated with PTSD symptoms [162, 163]. In the aforementioned study, Stein et al. found a significant association between childhood maltreatment, as measured by the Childhood Trauma Questionnaire (CTQ), and 5-HTTLPR genotype. More specifically, homozygotes with the *S* allele who also had a higher degree of maltreatment exhibited higher AS scores compared to heterozygotes and homozygous *L* carriers. Based on this association, the authors of the Stein study suggest that anxiety sensitivity may represent an intermediate phenotype for anxiety, depression, and their co-morbidity [160].

FKBP5

FKBP5 is a co-chaperone protein that interacts with hsp90, a molecular chaperone itself, that maintains neuronal viability and binds to the glucocorticoid receptor (GR; [164]). FKBP5 also regulates GR sensitivity [165] and is part of the mature GR heterocomplex [166]. When hormone binds to the GR complex, FKBP5 is replaced by FKBP4, which through the recruitment of dynein, initiates nuclear translocation of the receptor complex. The intranuclear GR complex then regulates expression of glucocorticoid-responsive genes by functioning as a transcription factor [167]. The role of FKBP5 in glucocorticoid receptor feedback sensitivity is illustrated in Figure 3.

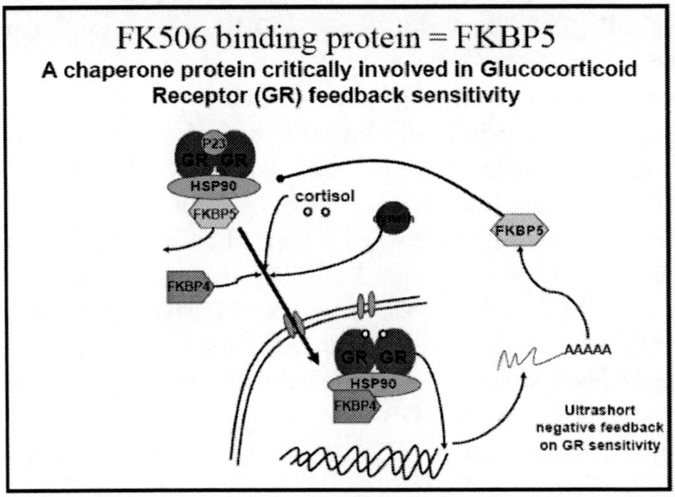

Figure 4. Schematic illustration of the role of FKBP5 in glucocorticoid receptor feedback sensitivity.

As part of the largest genetic study of PTSD to date, Binder et al. (2008), examined the association between FKBP5 polymorphisms and past child abuse on one's susceptibility to developing PTSD [168]. Four single nucleotide polymorphisms (SNPs) of the *FKBP5* gene (rs9296158, rs3800373, rs1360780, and rs9470080) significantly interacted with child abuse severity (as measured by the traumatic events inventory) to predict adult PTSD symptoms (as measured by the PTSD Symptom Scale). *FKBP5* polymorphisms were not significantly associated with PTSD symptoms and did not interact with past non–child abuse which suggests a putative gene x childhood-rearing environment interaction underlying vulnerability to adult PTSD.

Dopamine Beta-Hydroxylase

PTSD pathophysiology may also reflect altered dopaminergic and noradrenergic neurotransmission [169-171]. Genetic variants of the dopamine beta-hydroxylase gene (*DBH*) represent a likely candidate for examining genetic contributions to anxiety disorders because of the role this enzyme plays in converting dopamine to norepinephrine as part of catecholamine synthesis [172]. Plasma DBH activity is regulated by genetic factors [173]. More specifically, individual differences in DBH activity (approximately 35-52% of the variance) are influenced by a single nucleotide polymorphism (SNP) in the 5' flanking region of *DBH*, -1021C/T (rs1611115; [174]). Based on this degree of genetic influence on DBH activity, studies of plasma DBH activity should account for the rs1611115 genotype [173, 175]. In one such study, Mustapic et al. (2007) reported no significant difference in DBH genotype or allele frequency between a population of Croatian war veterans with PTSD and veterans without PTSD. However, the authors found an interaction effect between combat history, PTSD status, and genotype such that war veterans with PTSD who carried the CC genotype of the *DBH*-1021C/T variant had lower plasma DBH activity. Mustapic and others suggest that genotype-mediated plasma DBH activity may serve as a biomarker for an individual's response to trauma (ie., vulnerability to developing PTSD).

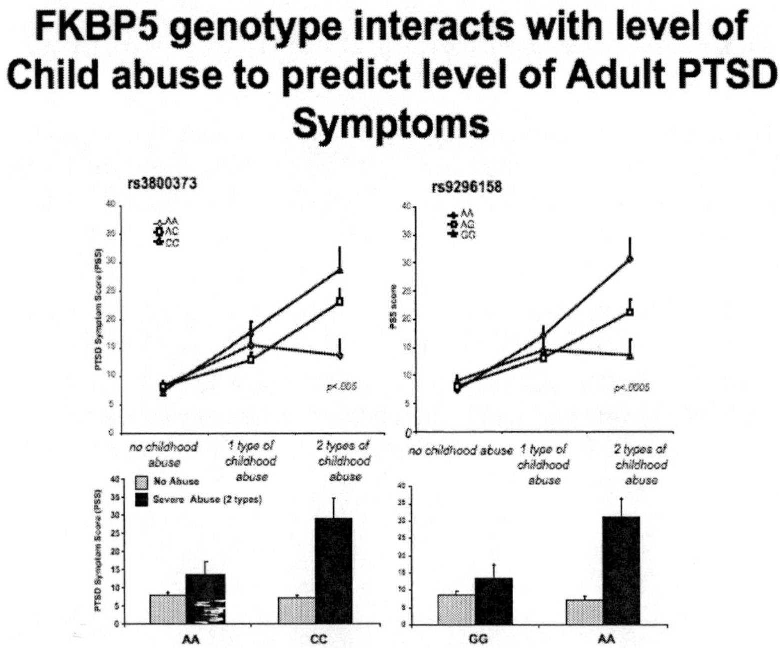

Figure 5. The rare alleles of the rs3800373 (CC) and rs9296158 (AA) SNPs of the *FKBP5* gene interacted with higher levels of childhood abuse to predict adult PTSD symptomatology. Adapted from Binder et al., 2008.

Attempts to identify predictive polymorphic variations in single loci have not led to any major discoveries regarding the genetic basis of PTSD. In general, these genetic association studies have revealed that (1) it is unlikely that specific anxiety disorders are associated with a single genetic variant, (2) there is a complex interaction between genetic and environmental factors, and (3) many of the identified genetic polymorphisms are in the regulatory promoter regions and not necessarily in the coding regions [13, 144]. Thus, future investigations aimed at identifying genetic contributions to PTSD will examine multiple susceptibility loci (including total genome analyses [176]) and will employ expanded gene x environment investigations.

Resilience Factors

Resilience has been defined as an individual's ability to cope with the effects of stress in a manner that is dependent on the context of the stressor, the duration of the stressor, an individual's age, an individual's gender, and cultural framework [177]. The underlying factors governing one's resilience in the face of stress include many that are neurobiological, temperamental, environmental, and genetic. Neurobiological determinants of resilience have been discussed in terms of "allostatic load [178]." McEwen and Stellar (1993) described allostatic load as the burden placed on neural and physiological systems as a result of the failure of homeostatic mechanisms to "reset" after stress exposure. Due to the limited focus of our review on the genetics of anxiety (and resilience), please see review work by McEwen and Stellar (1993) [178] as well as Charney (2004)[145]. An example of temperamental determinants of resilience can be found in a study by Tschann and others [179].

The genetic basis of resilience to stress has only recently been investigated. As discussed above, given the complexity of anxiety disorders such as PTSD, it is unlikely that these psychiatric illnesses are the result of single genetic variants. It is much more apparent to researchers and clinicians that vulnerability to PTSD and resilience to stress are the result of an interaction between genes and environment. Early work on the genetic basis of individual differences in stress responsivity was focused on the serotonin transporter gene (*SLC6A4*). Lesch and colleagues (1996, 1998) reported that the shorter *S* allele of the promoter region of *5-HTTLPR* was linked to decreased expression and activity of the serotonin transporter and anxiety traits in humans [134, 180]. In addition, individuals who are either homozygous or heterozygous for the *S* allele of 5-HTTLPR were more reactive, at the level of the amygdala, to fear-related stimuli as compared to those individuals who were homozygous for the longer *L* allele [181]. Hariri et al. (2002), Hamer (2002), as well as Connor and Zhang (2006) have emphasized the interpretation of these findings in the context of environmental influences such as education, socioeconomic status, family groups, and social support [170, 177, 181].

With regard to future gene x environment investigations of PTSD, it is clear that several factors need to be addressed when assessing the contributions of each to the anxiety-related phenotype that is expressed. In two previously described studies, environmental factors such as level of social support and child abuse history interacted with specific genetic polymorphisms to increase one's susceptibility to PTSD after trauma exposure. Resilience represents an additional environmental factor that could be studied further in ongoing gene x environment studies and could be ascertained through a number of measures including the Connor-Davidson Resilience Scale [182]. The primary factors that appear to mediate one's susceptibility versus resilience to PTSD following exposure to trauma are illustrated in Figure 6.

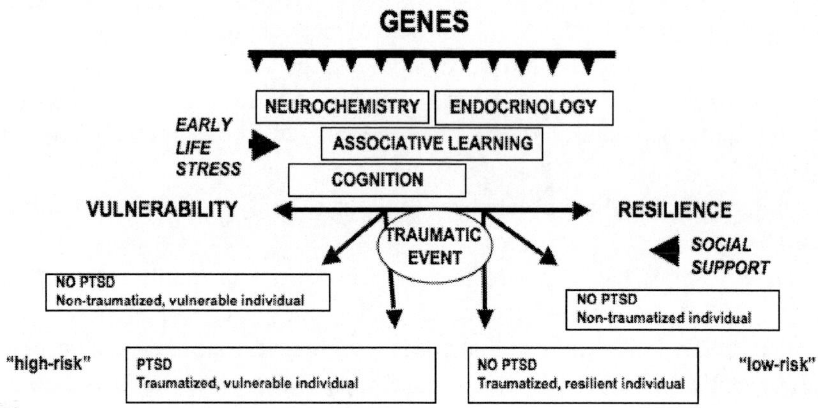

Figure 6. Diagram of genetic and environmental factors impacting vulnerability to develop PTSD after traumatic event. Individuals with putative vulnerability factors such as genetic polymorphisms and/or early life stress appear to be at higher risk for developing PTSD following trauma exposure as compared to individuals with putative resiliency factors including social support.

PTSD and Co-morbidity with Major Depressive Disorder: Common Genetic Liability

Evidence suggests that PTSD is more than simply a disorder characterized by impaired fear processing. PTSD is highly co-morbid with other psychiatric illnesses including mood disorders such as major depressive disorder [141]. It has been suggested that susceptibility to anxiety disorders is associated with increased risk for mood disorders and vice versa [183]; however, this relationship has not been fully investigated with PTSD and depression. Breslau and colleagues (1998) found that pre-existing depression is a risk factor for experiencing a traumatic event as well as developing PTSD after trauma exposure [184]. In addition, the development of depression after a traumatic event is more frequent in individuals with PTSD as compared to traumatized individuals without PTSD [185]. The accumulating literature suggests common genetic susceptibility factors for the development of PTSD and major depression. For example, Koenen et al. (2007) calculated that a majority of the genetic variance in PTSD is the result of co-morbid major depression [138]. In addition, the homozygous *S* polymorphism of the serotonin transporter has been associated with both PTSD and major depression [158, 159]. If there are indeed common genetic influences on PTSD and major depression and their co-morbidity, future studies must address the environmental factors that mediate which phenotypes are actually expressed clinically in at-risk individuals.

Epigenetics

The genetic contribution to the complex phenotypes associated with anxiety disorders and the co-morbid psychiatric conditions with which they cluster may be best explained by epigenetic phenomena. These phenomena are functional alterations to the genome that (1) are transmissible, (2) are affected by environmental factors, and (3) do not involve changes to the genetic sequence [186]. As previously described, histone modification is a fundamental process underlying epigenetic regulation and typically involves posttranslational alterations including methylation, phosphorylation, and acetylation at specific residues including arginine, histidine, lysine, serine, and threonine [187].

Vulnerability to PTSD, as an example, may be the result of individual differences that are defined by environmentally-induced alterations in gene expression [188]. Rodent studies have provided some evidence of the mechanism by which epigenetic factors may predispose an individual to PTSD. As shown by Francis and colleagues (1999) and other groups, early life stress (e.g., maternal deprivation) can have long-lasting effects on HPA axis function [189]. It was recently shown that DNA methylation serves as an underlying mechanism for persistent early life stress-induced HPA alterations [190]. A very recent study by Yehuda and others (2008) implicated epigenetic mechanisms as underlying the observation that PTSD prevalence was found to be higher in the children of Holocaust survivors with PTSD as compared to controls. In the latter study, maternal PTSD diagnosis, and not paternal PTSD, was associated with greater risk for developing PTSD after trauma exposure [191]. In the same study, PTSD diagnosis in *either* parent was linked to depression in the offspring while trauma exposure in *either* parent was linked to anxiety disorder diagnosis in the offspring. Although the specific mechanisms are unexplained, these findings suggest that some risk factors for depression and anxiety may be transmitted through classic genetic means whereas other risk factors may influence phenotypic expression through epigenetic means.

Chapter 7

FUTURE DIRECTIONS

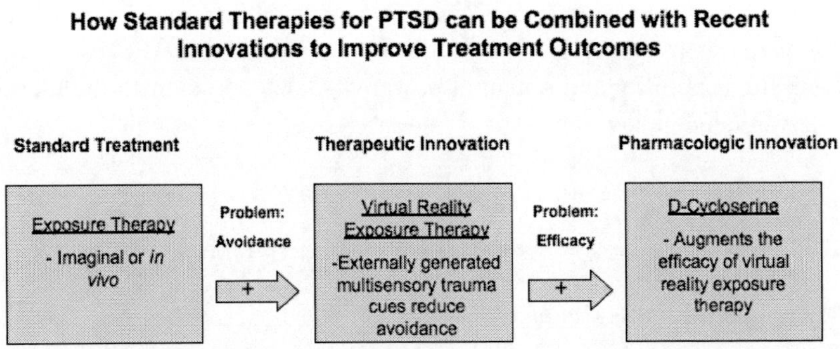

Figure 7. Recent advances in translational clinical research methodologies have provided clinicians with innovative strategies for addressing obstacles to favorable treatment outcomes such as patient avoidance.

As described above, translational clinical studies have informed several clinical applications for treating combat-related PTSD. From a pharmacological perspective, there may be a movement toward facilitating extinction learning through the adjunct administration of cognitive enhancers such as DCS. Technologically speaking, VR may represent an important additional treatment approach that can augment extant cognitive behavioral therapies in that it provides more precise control over stimulus exposure across multiple sensory modalities (e.g., sight, sound, smell). Thus, VR may be associated with a higher degree of emotional engagement with the trauma memory. VR also allows for the concurrent assessment of psychophysiological measures such as heart rate, respiration, and skin conductance; measures that can provide clinicians with increased evidence for gauging treatment responses over time. Emerging pilot studies have shown the coupling of VR technology with psychophysiological recording systems to be a promising new application as comprehensive treatment programs for War on Terror-related PTSD are developed [192]. Figure 7 demonstrates the manner in which emerging translational findings can impact treatment decisions related to combat PTSD. As shown in the figure, virtual reality is often an attractive alternative to imaginal exposure therapy, most notably in patients that suffer from symptoms of avoidance. In addition, augmentation of exposure therapy with DCS provides clinicians with a practical alternative for improving the efficacy of traditional exposure therapy regimens. From a genetics perspective, genome wide association studies (GWAS) are slowly emerging in a deliberate effort to address many of the limitations inherent with investigations of specific candidate genes. It is clear from the few reports that have surfaced recently that much work remains to be done. However, early results have illustrated the feasibility and potential power of GWAS to identify biomarkers for anxiety-related behaviors.

Conclusion

Key points from this Chapter:

1. The symptoms of PTSD are characterized by both emotional and fear processing elements
2. Traditional pharmacological treatments (e.g., SSRIs) have focused on symptoms related to emotional quality of life whereas future drugs may be targeted toward the fear-related aspects of the disorder (e.g., d-cycloserine coupled with exposure therapy)
3. Virtual reality represents an attractive alternative to traditional imaginal exposure therapy for refractory or previously untreated cases
4. No clear genetic basis for PTSD has been identified; it appears to the result of a complex gene x environment interaction
5. This, the identification of risk and resiliency factors in an individual's history may improve both the diagnosis (and potential prophylaxes) and treatments for combat-related PTSD

REFERENCES

[1] Hoge CW, Castro CA, Messer SC, McGurk D, Cotting DI, Koffman RL. Combat duty in Iraq and Afghanistan, mental health problems, and barriers to care. *The New England journal of medicine*. 2004 Jul 1;351(1):13-22.

[2] Plowshares P. Armed Conflicts Report Summary 2008. Project Plowshares 2008 [cited; Available from: http://www.ploughshares.ca/libraries/ACRText/Summary2007.pdf

[3] Hoge CW, McGurk D, Thomas JL, Cox AL, Engel CC, Castro CA. Mild traumatic brain injury in U.S. Soldiers returning from Iraq. *The New England journal of medicine*. 2008 Jan 31;358(5):453-63.

[4] APA. *Diagnostic and statistical manual of mental disorders (DSM-IV)*. 4 ed. Washington, D.C.: American Psychiatric Association 1994.

[5] Ursano RJ, Bell C, Eth S, Friedman M, Norwood A, Pfefferbaum B, et al. Practice guideline for the treatment of patients with acute stress disorder and posttraumatic stress disorder. *The American journal of psychiatry*. 2004 Nov;161(11 Suppl):3-31.

[6] Blake DD, Weathers FW, Nagy LM, Kaloupek DG, Gusman FD, Charney DS, et al. The development of a Clinician-Administered PTSD Scale. *Journal of traumatic stress*. 1995 Jan;8(1):75-90.

[7] Guy W. *Assessment Manual for Psychopharmacology - Revised* Rockville, MD: U.S. Department of Health, Education, and Welfare, Public Health Service, Alcohol, Drug Abuse, and Mental Health Administration, NIMH Psychopharmacology Research Branch, Division of Extramural Research Program 1976.

[8] Rothbaum BO, Davis M. Applying learning principles to the treatment of post-trauma reactions. *Annals of the New York Academy of Sciences*. 2003;1008:112-21.

[9] Ursano RJ, Zhang L, Li H, Johnson L, Carlton J, Fullerton CS, et al. PTSD and traumatic stress: From gene to community and bench to bedside. *Brain research*. 2009;Epub.

[10] Foa EB, Zinbarg R, Rothbaum BO. Uncontrollability and unpredictability in post-traumatic stress disorder: an animal model. *Psychological bulletin*. 1992 Sep;112(2):218-38.

[11] Servatius RJ, Beck KD, Moldow RL, Salameh G, Tumminello TP, Short KR. A stress-induced anxious state in male rats: corticotropin-releasing hormone induces persistent changes in associative learning and startle reactivity. *Biological psychiatry*. 2005 Apr 15;57(8):865-72.

[12] Servatius RJ, Ottenweller JE, Natelson BH. Delayed startle sensitization distinguishes rats exposed to one or three stress sessions: further evidence toward an animal model of PTSD. *Biological psychiatry*. 1995 Oct 15;38(8):539-46.

[13] Smoller JW, Gardner-Schuster E, Covino J. The genetic basis of panic and phobic anxiety disorders. *American journal of medical genetics, part C Seminars in Medical Genetics.* 2008 May 15;148(2):118-26.

[14] Foa EB, Steketee G, Rothbaum BO. Behavioral/cognitive conceptualizations of post-traumatic stress disorder. *Behavioral therapy.* 1989;20:155-76.

[15] Miller MM, McEwen BS. Establishing an agenda for translational research on PTSD. *Annals of the New York academy of sciences*. 2006;1071:294-312.

[16] Landis C, Hunt W. *The startle pattern*. New York, NY: Farrar and Rinehart 1939.

[17] Davis M. The mammalian startle response. In: Eaton RC, ed. *Neural mechanisms of startle behavior*. New York, NY: Plenum Press 1984:287-351.

[18] Jovanovic T, Norrholm SD, Fennell JE, Keyes M, Fiallos A, Myers KM, et al. Posttraumatic stress disorder may be associated with impaired fear inhibition: relation to symptom severity. *Psychiatry research*. 2008;in press.

[19] Norrholm SD, Jovanovic T, Vervliet B, Myers KM, Davis M, Rothbaum BO, et al. Conditioned fear extinction and reinstatement in a human fear-potentiated startle paradigm. *Learning & memory*. 2006;13(6):681-5.

[20] Grillon C. Startle reactivity and anxiety disorders: aversive conditioning, context, and neurobiology. *Biological psychiatry*. 2002 Nov 15;52(10):958-75.

[21] Graham F. The more or less startling effects of weak prestimulus. *Psychophysiology*. 1975;12:238-48.

[22] Lang PJ, Bradley MM, Cuthbert BN. Emotion, attention, and the startle reflex. *Psychology review*. 1990;9:377-95.

[23] Davis M, Falls WA, Campeau S, Kim M. Fear-potentiated startle: a neural and pharmacological analysis. *Behavioural brain research*. 1993 Dec 20;58(1-2):175-98.

[24] Grillon C, Baas J. A review of the modulation of the startle reflex by affective states and its application in psychiatry. *Clinical neurophysiology*. 2003 Sep;114(9):1557-79.

[25] Davis M. The role of the amygdala in fear and anxiety. *Annual reviews in neuroscience*. 1992;15:353-75.

[26] Davis M. Differential roles of the amygdala and bed nucleus of the stria terminalis in conditioned fear and startle enhanced by corticotropin releasing hormone. In: Ono T, McNaughton BL, Nishijo H, eds. *Perception, memory, and emotion: frontiers in neuroscience*. Oxford: Elsevier 1996:525-48.

[27] Davis M. The Neurophysiological Basis of Acoustic Startle Modulation: Research on Fear Motivation and Sensory Gating. In: Lang PJ, Simons RF, Balaban MT, eds. *Attention and Orienting: Sensory and Motivational Processes*. Mahwah, NJ: Lawrence Erlbaum Associates 1997:69-96.

[28] Davis M, Gendelman DS, Tischler MD, Gendelman PM. A primary acoustic startle circuit: lesion and stimulation studies. *J neuroscience*. 1982 Jun;2(6):791-805.

[29] Koch M. The neurobiology of startle. *Progress in neurobiology*. 1999 Oct;59(2):107-28.

[30] Lang PJ, Davis M, Ohman A. Fear and anxiety: animal models and human cognitive psychophysiology. *Journal of affective disorders*. 2000 Dec;61(3):137-59.

[31] Lee Y, Lopez DE, Meloni EG, Davis M. A primary acoustic startle pathway: obligatory role of cochlear root neurons and the nucleus reticularis pontis caudalis. *Journal of neuroscience*. 1996 Jun 1;16(11):3775-89.

[32] Dawson ME, Schell AM, Bomehlt AH. Startle modification: introduction and overview. In: Dawson ME, Schell AM, Bomehlt AH, eds. *Startle modification Implications for neuroscience, cognitive science, and clinical science*. Cambridge: Cambridge University Press 1999:6-18.

[33] Davis M, Walker DL, Lee Y. Neurophysiology and neuropharmacology of startle and its affective modulation. In: Dawson ME, Schell AM, Bomehlt AH, eds. *Startle modificaton Implications for neuroscience, cognitive science, and clinical science*. Cambridge: Cambridge University Press 1999:95-113.

[34] Wagner AR, Logan FA, Haberlandt K, Price T. Stimulus selection in animal discrimination learning. *Journal of experimental psychology*. 1968;76:171-80.

[35] Myers KM, Davis M. AX+, BX- discrimination learning in the fear-potentiated startle paradigm: possible relevance to inhibitory fear learning in extinction. *Learning & memory*. 2004 Jul-Aug;11(4):464-75.

[36] Jovanovic T, Norrholm SD, Fiallos A, Keyes M, Myers K, Davis M, et al. Fear potentiation and fear inhibition in PTSD. Extinction: The Neural Mechanisms of Behavior Change; 2005; Ponce, Puerto Rico; 2005.

[37] Rothbaum BO, Meadows EA, Resick P, Foy DW. Cognitive-Behavioral Therapy. In: Foa EB, Friedman MI, Keane T, eds. *Effective treatments for posttraumatic stress disorder: practice guidelines from the International Society for Traumatic Stress Studies*: Guilford Press 2000:60-83.

[38] Pavlov IP. *Conditioned Reflexes*. Oxford University Press 1927.

[39] Davis M, Ressler K, Rothbaum BO, Richardson R. Effects of d-cycloserine on extinction: translation from preclinical to clinical work. *Biological psychiatry*. 2006;60(4):369-75.

[40] Rothbaum BO, Kozak MJ, Foa EB, Whitaker DJ. Posttraumatic stress disorder in rape victims: autonomic habituation to auditory stimuli. *Journal of traumatic stress*. 2001 Apr;14(2):283-93.

[41] Blechert J, Michael T, Vriends N, Wilhelm FH. Fear conditioning in posttraumatic stress disorder: Evidence for delayed extinction of autonomic, experiential, and behavioral responses. *Behaviour research and therapy*. 2007 March 12, 2007;Epub.

[42] Guthrie RM, Bryant RA. Extinction learning before trauma and subsequent posttraumatic stress. *Psychosomatic medicine*. 2006;68:307-11.

[43] Wessa M, Flor H. Failure of extinction of fear responses in posttraumatic stress disorder: evidence from second-order conditioning. *The American journal of psychiatry*. 2007;164(11):1684-92.

[44] Zoladz PR, Conrad CD, Fleshner M, Diamond DM. Acute episodes of predator exposure in conjunction with chronic social instability as an

animal model of post-traumatic stress disorder. *Stress* (Amsterdam, Netherlands). 2008;11(4):259-81.

[45] Huhman KL. Social conflict models: can they inform us about human psychopathology? *Hormones and behavior*. 2006 Nov;50(4):640-6.

[46] Belda X, Rotllant D, Fuentes S, Delgado R, Nadal R, Armario A. Exposure to severe stressors causes long-lasting dysregulation of resting and stress-induced activation of the hypothalamic-pituitary-adrenal axis. *Annals of the New York academy of sciences*. 2008 Dec;1148:165-73.

[47] Borcel E, Perez-Alvarez L, Herrero AI, Brionne T, Varea E, Berezin V, et al. Chronic stress in adulthood followed by intermittent stress impairs spatial memory and the survival of newborn hippocampal cells in aging animals: prevention by FGL, a peptide mimetic of neural cell adhesion molecule. *Behavioural pharmacology*. 2008 Feb;19(1):41-9.

[48] Ursano RJ, Li H, Zhang L, Hough CJ, Fullerton CS, Benedek DM, et al. Models of PTSD and traumatic stress: the importance of research "from bedside to bench to bedside". *Progress in brain research*. 2008;167:203-15.

[49] Bradley R, Greene J, Russ E, Dutra L, Westen D. A multidimensional meta-analysis of psychotherapy for PTSD. *The American journal of psychiatry*. 2005;162(2):214-27.

[50] Medicine Io. Treatment of posttraumatic stress disorder: An assessment of the evidence. 2008 [cited 2007 October]; Available from: http://nap.edu/catalog.php?record_id=11955#toc

[51] Foa EB, Kozak MJ. Emotional processing of fear: exposure to corrective information. *Psychological bulletin*. 1986 Jan;99(1):20-35.

[52] Foa EB, Hembree E, Rothbaum BO. *Prolonged Exposure Therapy for PTSD: Emotional Processing of Traumatic Experiences, Therapist Guide*. New York, NY: Oxford University Press 2007.

[53] Van Etten ML, Taylor S. Comparative efficacy of treatments for post-traumatic stress disorder: A meta-analysis. *Clinical psychology and psychotherapy*. 1998;5:126-44.

[54] Rothbaum BO, Hodges L, Smith S, Lee JH, Price L. A controlled study of virtual reality exposure therapy for the fear of flying. *Journal of consulting and clinical psychology*. 2000 Dec;68(6):1020-6.

[55] Foa EB, Keane TM, Friedman MJ. *Effective treatments for PTSD: practice guidelines from the International Society for Traumatic Stress Studies*. New York: Guilford Press 2000.

[56] Foa EB, Huppert JD, Cahill SP. Emotional processing theory: an update. In: Rothbaum BO, ed. *Pathological anxiety*. New York, NY: Guilford Press 2006:3-24.

[57] Difede J, Cukor J, Jayasinghe N, Patt I, Jedel S, Spielman L, et al. Virtual reality exposure therapy for the treatment of posttraumatic stress disorder following September 11, 2001. *The Journal of clinical psychiatry*. 2007 Nov;68(11):1639-47.

[58] Rothbaum BO, Hodges LF, Ready D, Graap K, Alarcon RD. Virtual reality exposure therapy for Vietnam veterans with posttraumatic stress disorder. *The Journal of clinical psychiatry*. 2001 Aug;62(8):617-22.

[59] Reger GM, Gahm GA, Rizzo AA, Swanson R, Duma S. Soldier evaluation of the virtual reality Iraq. *Telemedicine journal and e-health*. 2009 Jan;15(1):101-4.

[60] Gerardi M, Rothbaum BO, Ressler K, Heekin M, Rizzo A. Virtual reality exposure therapy using a virtual Iraq: case report. *Journal of traumatic stress*. 2008 Apr;21(2):209-13.

[61] Stein DJ, Ipser J, McAnda N. Pharmacotherapy of posttraumatic stress disorder: a review of meta-analyses and treatment guidelines. *CNS spectrums*. 2009 Jan;14(1 Suppl 1):25-31.

[62] Berger W, Mendlowicz MV, Marques-Portella C, Kinrys G, Fontenelle LF, Marmar CR, et al. Pharmacologic alternatives to antidepressants in posttraumatic stress disorder: A systematic review. *Progress in neuro-psychopharmacology & biological psychiatry*. 2009 Mar 17;33(2):169-80.

[63] Zohar J, Amital D, Miodownik C, Kotler M, Bleich A, Lane RM, et al. Double-blind placebo-controlled pilot study of sertraline in military veterans with posttraumatic stress disorder. *Journal of clinical psychopharmacology*. 2002 Apr;22(2):190-5.

[64] Stein MB, Kline NA, Matloff JL. Adjunctive olanzapine for SSRI-resistant combat-related PTSD: a double-blind, placebo-controlled study. *The American journal of psychiatry*. 2002 Oct;159(10):1777-9.

[65] U.S. Department of Health and Human Services Dgp. *Clinical practice guideline No.5: depression in primary care*. Rockville, MD: AHCPR Publications 1993.

[66] Padala PR, Madison J, Monnahan M, Marcil W, Price P, Ramaswamy S, et al. Risperidone monotherapy for post-traumatic stress disorder related to sexual assault and domestic abuse in women. *International clinical psychopharmacology*. 2006 Sep;21(5):275-80.

[67] Kozaric-Kovacic D, Pivac N, Muck-Seler D, Rothbaum BO. Rispiridone in psychotic combat-related posttraumatic stress disorder: an open trial. *The Journal of clinical psychiatry*. 2005;66:922-7.

[68] Bartzokis G, Lu PH, Turner J, Mintz J, Saunders CS. Adjunctive risperidone in the treatment of chronic combat-related posttraumatic stress disorder. *Biological psychiatry*. 2005 Mar 1;57(5):474-9.

[69] Monnelly EP, Ciraulo DA, Knapp C, Keane T. Low-dose risperidone as adjunctive therapy for irritable aggression in posttraumatic stress disorder. *Journal of clinical psychopharmacology*. 2003 Apr;23(2):193-6.

[70] Reich DB, Winternitz S, Hennen J, Watts T, Stanculescu C. A preliminary study of risperidone in the treatment of posttraumatic stress disorder related to childhood abuse in women. *The Journal of clinical psychiatry*. 2004 Dec;65(12):1601-6.

[71] David D, De Faria L, Lapeyra O, Mellman TA. Adjunctive risperidone treatment in combat veterans with chronic PTSD. *Journal of clinical psychopharmacology*. 2004 Oct;24(5):556-9.

[72] Hamner MB, Faldowski RA, Ulmer HG, Frueh BC, Huber MG, Arana GW. Adjunctive risperidone treatment in post-traumatic stress disorder: a preliminary controlled trial of effects on comorbid psychotic symptoms. *International clinical psychopharmacology*. 2003 Jan;18(1):1-8.

[73] Rothbaum BO, Killeen TK, Davidson JR, Brady KT, Connor KM, Heekin MH. Placebo-controlled trial of risperidone augmentation for selective serotonin reuptake inhibitor-resistant civilian posttraumatic stress disorder. *The Journal of clinical psychiatry*. 2008 Apr;69(4):520-5.

[74] Petty F, Brannan S, Casada J, Davis LL, Gajewski V, Kramer GL, et al. Olanzapine treatment for post-traumatic stress disorder: an open-label study. *International clinical psychopharmacology*. 2001 Nov;16(6):331-7.

[75] Butterfield MI, Becker ME, Connor KM, Sutherland S, Churchill LE, Davidson JR. Olanzapine in the treatment of post-traumatic stress disorder: a pilot study. *International clinical psychopharmacology*. 2001 Jul;16(4):197-203.

[76] Jakovljevic M, Sagud M, Mihaljevic-Peles A. Olanzapine in the treatment resistant, combat-related PTSD-a series of case reports. *Acta psychiatrica Scandinavica*. 2003;107:394-6.

[77] States HS, St. Dennis CD. Chronic sleep disruption and the reexperiencing cluster of posttraumatic stress disorder symptomes are improved by olanzapine: brief review of the literature and a case-based series. *Primary care companion journal of clinical psychiatry*. 2003;5:74-9.

[78] Davis LL, Davidson JR, Ward LC, Bartolucci A, Bowden CL, Petty F. Divalproex in the treatment of posttraumatic stress disorder: a randomized, double-blind, placebo-controlled trial in a veteran population. *Journal of clinical psychopharmacology*. 2008 Feb;28(1):84-8.

[79] Steiner H, Saxena KS, Carrion V, Khanzode LA, Silverman M, Chang K. Divalproex sodium for the treatment of PTSD and conduct disordered youth: a pilot randomized controlled clinical trial. *Child psychiatry and human development*. 2007 Oct;38(3):183-93.

[80] Clark RD, Canive JM, Calais LA, Qualls CR, Tuason VB. Divalproex in posttraumatic stress disorder: an open-label clinical trial. *Journal of traumatic stress*. 1999 Apr;12(2):395-401.

[81] Petty F, Davis LL, Nugent AL, Kramer GL, Teten A, Schmitt A, et al. Valproate therapy for chronic, combat-induced posttraumatic stress disorder. *Journal of clinical psychopharmacology*. 2002 Feb;22(1):100-1.

[82] Goldberg JF, Cloitre M, Whiteside JE, Han H. An open-label pilot study of divalproex sodium for posttraumatic stress disorder related to childhood abuse. *Current therapeutic research, clinical and experimental*. 2003;64:45-54.

[83] Fesler FA. Valproate in combat-related posttraumatic stress disorder. *The Journal of clinical psychiatry*. 1991 Sep;52(9):361-4.

[84] Raskind MA, Peskind ER, Hoff DJ, Hart KL, Holmes HA, Warren D, et al. A parallel group placebo controlled study of prazosin for trauma nightmares and sleep disturbance in combat veterans with post-traumatic stress disorder. *Biological psychiatry*. 2007 Apr 15;61(8):928-34.

[85] Debiec J, LeDoux JE. Noradrenergic signaling in the amygdala contributes to the reconsolidation of fear memory: treatment implications for PTSD. *Annals of the New York Academy of sciences*. 2006 Jul;1071:521-4.

[86] Shin LM, Rauch SL, Pitman RK. Amygdala, medial prefrontal cortex, and hippocampal function in PTSD. *Annals of the New York Academy of sciences*. 2006 Jul;1071:67-79.

[87] Taylor FB, Martin P, Thompson C, Williams J, Mellman TA, Gross C, et al. Prazosin effects on objective sleep measures and clinical symptoms in civilian trauma posttraumatic stress disorder: a placebo-controlled study. *Biological psychiatry*. 2008 Mar 15;63(6):629-32.

[88] Raskind MA, Peskind ER, Kanter ED, Petrie EC, Radant A, Thompson CE, et al. Reduction of nightmares and other PTSD symptoms in combat veterans by prazosin: a placebo-controlled study. *The American journal of psychiatry*. 2003 Feb;160(2):371-3.

[89] Taylor FB, Lowe K, Thompson C, McFall MM, Peskind ER, Kanter ED, et al. Daytime prazosin reduces psychological distress to trauma specific cues in civilian trauma posttraumatic stress disorder. *Biological psychiatry*. 2006 Apr 1;59(7):577-81.

[90] Peskind ER, Bonner LT, Hoff DJ, Raskind MA. Prazosin reduces trauma-related nightmares in older men with chronic posttraumatic stress disorder. *Journal of geriatric psychiatry and neurology*. 2003 Sep;16(3):165-71.

[91] Raskind MA, Thompson C, Petrie EC, Dobie DJ, Rein RJ, Hoff DJ, et al. Prazosin reduces nightmares in combat veterans with posttraumatic stress disorder. *The Journal of clinical psychiatry*. 2002 Jul;63(7):565-8.

[92] Daly CM, Doyle ME, Radkind M, Raskind E, Daniels C. Clinical case series: the use of Prazosin for combat-related recurrent nightmares among Operation Iraqi Freedom combat veterans. *Military medicine*. 2005 Jun;170(6):513-5.

[93] Taylor F, Raskind MA. The alpha1-adrenergic antagonist prazosin improves sleep and nightmares in civilian trauma posttraumatic stress disorder. *Journal of clinical psychopharmacology*. 2002 Feb;22(1):82-5.

[94] Newcomer JW, Krystal JH. NMDA receptor regulation of memory and behavior in humans. *Hippocampus*. 2001;11(5):529-42.

[95] Morris RG, Davis S, Butcher SP. Hippocampal synaptic plasticity and NMDA receptors: a role in information storage? *Philosophical transactions of the Royal Society of London*. 1990 Aug 29;329(1253):187-204.

[96] Castellano C, Cestari V, Ciamei A. NMDA receptors and learning and memory processes. *Current drug targets*. 2001 Sep;2(3):273-83.

[97] Bear MF. A synaptic basis for memory storage in the cerebral cortex. *Proceedings of the National Academy of Sciences of the United States of America*. 1996 Nov 26;93(24):13453-9.

[98] Miserendino MJ, Sananes CB, Melia KR, Davis M. Blocking of acquisition but not expression of conditioned fear-potentiated startle by

NMDA antagonists in the amygdala. *Nature*. 1990 Jun 21;345(6277):716-8.

[99] Falls WA, Miserendino MJ, Davis M. Extinction of fear-potentiated startle: blockade by infusion of an NMDA antagonist into the amygdala. *Journal of neuroscience*. 1992 Mar;12(3):854-63.

[100] Kehoe EJ, Macrae M, Hutchinson CL. MK-801 protects conditioned response from extinction in the rabbit nictitating membrane preparation. *Psychobiology*. 1996;24:127-35.

[101] Szapiro G, Vianna MR, McGaugh JL, Medina JH, Izquierdo I. The role of NMDA glutamate receptors, PKA, MAPK, and CamKIII in the hippocampus in extinction of conditioned fear. *Hippocampus*. 2003;13:53-8.

[102] Lee H, Kim JJ. Amygdalar NMDA receptors are critical for new fear learning in previously fear-conditioned rats. *Journal of neuroscience*. 1998 Oct 15;18(20):8444-54.

[103] Walker DL, Ressler KJ, Lu KT, Davis M. Facilitation of conditioned fear extinction by systemic administration or intra-amygdala infusions of D-cycloserine as assessed with fear-potentiated startle in rats. *Journal of neuroscience*. 2002 Mar 15;22(6):2343-51.

[104] Ledgerwood L, Richardson R, Cranney J. Effects of D-cycloserine on extinction of conditioned freezing. *Behavioral neuroscience*. 2003;117(2):341-9.

[105] Yang YL, Lu KT. Facilitation of conditioned fear extinction by d-cycloserine is mediated by mitogen-activated protein kinase and phosphatidylinositol 3-kinase cascades and requires de novo protein synthesis in basolateral nucleus of amygdala. *Neuroscience*. 2005;134:247-60.

[106] Ledgerwood L, Richardson R, Cranney J. D-cycloserine facilitates extinction of learned fear: effects on reacquisition and generalized extinction. *Biological psychiatry*. 2005 Apr 15;57(8):841-7.

[107] Myers KM, Davis M. Behavioral and neural analysis of extinction. *Neuron*. 2002 Nov 14;36(4):567-84.

[108] Ledgerwood L, Richardson R, Cranney J. D-cycloserine and the facilitation of extinction of conditioned fear: consequences for reinstatement. *Behavioral neuroscience*. 2004;118(3):505-13.

[109] Heresco-Levy U, Kremer I, Javitt DC, Goichman R, Reshef A, Blanaru M, et al. Pilot-controlled trial of d-cycloserine for the treatment of post-traumatic stress disorder. *International journal of neuropsychopharmacology*. 2002;5:301-7.

[110] Ressler KJ, Rothbaum BO, Tannenbaum L, Anderson P, Graap K, Zimand E, et al. Cognitive enhancers as adjuncts to psychotherapy: use of D-cycloserine in phobic individuals to facilitate extinction of fear. *Archives of general psychiatry*. 2004 Nov;61(11):1136-44.

[111] Rothbaum BO, Hodges LF, Kooper R, Opdyke D, Williford JS, North M. Effectiveness of computer-generated (virtual reality) graded exposure in the treatment of acrophobia. *The American journal of psychiatry*. 1995 Apr;152(4):626-8.

[112] Hofmann SG, Meuret AE, Smits JAJ, Simon NM, Pollack MH, Eisenmenger K, et al. Augmentation of exposure therapy with d-cycloserine for social anxiety disorder. *Archives of general psychiatry*. 2006;63:298-304.

[113] Quartermain D, Mower J, Rafferty MF, Herting RL, Lanthorn TH. Acute but not chronic activation of the NMDA-coupled glycine receptor with D-cycloserine facilitates learning and retention. *European journal of pharmacology*. 1994 May 12;257(1-2):7-12.

[114] Parnas AS, Weber M, Richardson R. Effects of multiple exposures to D-cycloserine on extinction of conditioned fear in rats. *Neurobiology of learning and memory*. 2005;83(3):224-31.

[115] Yamamoto S, Morinobu S, Fuchikami M, Kurata A, Kozuru T, Yamawaki S. Effects of single prolonged stress and D-cycloserine on contextual fear extinction and hippocampal NMDA receptor expression in a rat model of PTSD. *Neuropsychopharmacology*. 2008;33(9):2108-16.

[116] Chhatwal JP, Davis M, Maguschak KA, Ressler KJ. Enhancing cannabinoid neurotransmission augments the extinction of conditioned fear. *Neuropsychopharmacology*. 2005;30:516-24.

[117] Chhatwal JP, Gutman AR, Maguschak KA, Bowser ME, Yang Y, Davis M, et al. Functional interactions between endocannabinoid and CCK neurotransmitter systems may be critical for extinction learning. *Neuropsychopharmacology*. 2009;34(2):509-21.

[118] Ramakrishnan V. Histone structure. *Current opinion in structural biology*. 1994;4:44-50.

[119] Adolph KW. *Chromosomes and chromatin*: CRC Press 1988.

[120] Levenson JM, O'Riordan KJ, Brown KD, Trinh MA, Molfese DL, Sweatt JD. Regulation of histone acetylation during memory formation in the hippocampus. The *Journal of biological chemistry*. 2004;279:40545-59.

[121] Martinowich K, Hattori D, Wu H, Fouse S, He F, Hu Y, et al. DNA methylation-related chromatin remodeling in activity-dependent BDNF gene regulation. *Science* (New York, NY. 2003;302:890-3.

[122] Bredy TW, Barad M. The histone deacetylase inhibitor valproic acid enhances acquisition, extinction, and reconsolidation of conditioned fear. *Learning & memory*. 2008.

[123] Bredy TW, Wu H, Crego C, Zellhoefer J, Sun YE, Barad M. Histone modifications around individual BDNF gene promoters in prefrontal cortex are associated with extinction of conditioned fear. *Learning & memory*. 2007;14:268-76.

[124] Lattal KM, Barrett RM, Wood MA. Systemic or intrahippocampal delivery of histone deacetylase inhibitors facilitates fear extinction. *Behavioral neuroscience*. 2007;121:1125-31.

[125] Vecsey CG, Hawk JD, Lattal KM, Stein JM, Fabian SA, Attner MA, et al. Histone deacetylase inhibitors enhance memory and synaptic plasticity via CREB:CBP-dependent transcriptional activation. *Journal of neuroscience*. 2007;6128-6140.

[126] Wood MA, Attner MA, Oliveira AM, Brindle PK, Abel T. A transcription factor-binding domain of the coactivator CBP is essential for long-term memory and the expression of specific target genes. *Learning & memory*. 2006;13:609-17.

[127] Yeh SH, Lin CH, Gean PW. Acetylation of nuclear factor-kB in rat amygdala improves long-term but not short-term retention of fear memory. *Molecular pharmacology*. 2004;65:1286-92.

[128] Chhatwal JP, Stanek-Rattiner L, Davis M, Ressler KJ. Amygdala BDNF signaling is required for consolidation but not encoding of extinction. *Nature neuroscience*. 2006;9:870-2.

[129] Ou LC, Gean PW. Regulation of amygdala-dependent learning by brain-derived neurotrophic factor is mediated by extracellular signal-related kinase and phosphotidylinositol-3-kinase. *Neuropsychopharmacology*. 2006;31:287-96.

[130] Rattiner LM, Davis M, French CT, Ressler KJ. Brain-derived neurotrophic factor and tyrosine kinase receptor B involvement in amygdala-dependent fear conditioning. *Journal of neuroscience*. 2004 May 19;24(20):4796-806.

[131] Tsankova NM, Kumar A, Nestler EJ. Histone modifications at gene promoter regions in rat hippocampus after acute and chronic electroconvulsive seizures. *Journal of neuroscience*. 2004;24:5603-10.

[132] Ramey-Hartung B, El-Mallakh RS, Reynolds KK. Pharmacogenetic testing in schizophrenia and posttraumatic stress disorder. *Clinics in laboratory medicine*. 2008 Dec;28(4):627-43.

[133] Heils A, Teufel A, Petri S, Stober G, Riederer P, Bengel D, et al. Allelic variation of human serotonin transporter gene expression. *Journal of neurochemistry*. 1996 Jun;66(6):2621-4.

[134] Lesch KP, Bengel D, Heils A, Sabol SZ, Greenberg BD, Petri S, et al. Association of anxiety-related traits with a polymorphism in the serotonin transporter gene regulatory region. *Science* (New York, NY. 1996 Nov 29;274(5292):1527-31.

[135] Bradley SL, Dodelzon K, Sandhu HK, Philibert RA. Relationship of serotonin transporter gene polymorphisms and haplotypes to mRNA transcription. *American journal of medical genetics part B, neuropsychiatric genetics*. 2005 Jul 5;136B(1):58-61.

[136] Philibert RA, Sandhu H, Hollenbeck N, Gunter T, Adams W, Madan A. The relationship of 5HTT (SLC6A4) methylation and genotype on mRNA expression and liability to major depression and alcohol dependence in subjects from the Iowa Adoption Studies. *American journal of medical genetics part B, neuropsychiatric genetics*. 2008 Jul 5;147B(5):543-9.

[137] Kilpatrick DG, Koenen KC, Ruggiero KJ, Acierno R, Galea S, Resnick HS, et al. The serotonin transporter genotype and social support and moderation of posttraumatic stress disorder and depression in hurricane-exposed adults. *The American journal of psychiatry*. 2007 Nov;164(11):1693-9.

[138] Koenen KC. Genetics of posttraumatic stress disorder: review and recommendations for future studies. *Journal of traumatic stress*. 2007;20(5):737-50.

[139] Broekman BFP, Olff M, Boer F. The genetic background to PTSD. *Neuroscience and biobehavioral reviews*. 2007;31:348-62.

[140] Breslau N, Kessler RC. The stessor criterion in DSM-IV posttraumatic stress disorder: an empirical investigation. *Biological psychiatry*. 2001;50:699-704.

[141] Kessler RC, Sonnega A, Bromet E, Hughes M, Nelson CB. Posttraumatic stress disorder in the National Comorbidity Survey. *Archives of general psychiatry*. 1995 Dec;52(12):1048-60.

[142] Adams RE, Boscarino JA. Predictors of PTSD and delayed PTSD after disaster: the impact of exposure and psychosocial resources. *The Journal of nervous and mental disease*. 2006;194:485-93.

[143] Segman RH, Shalev AY. Genetics of posttraumatic stress disorder. *CNS spectrums.* 2003 Sep;8(9):693-8.

[144] Poulton R, Andrews G, Millichamp J. Gene-environment interaction and the anxiety disorders. *European archives of psychiatry and clinical neuroscience*. 2008 Mar;258(2):65-8.

[145] Charney DS. Psychobiological mechanisms of resilience and vulnerability: implications for successful adaptation to extreme stress. *The American journal of psychiatry*. 2004;161:195-216.

[146] Rasmusson AM, Vythilingham M, Morgan CA, 3rd. The neuroendocrinology of posttraumatic stress disorder: new directions. *CNS spectrums*. 2003;8:651-7.

[147] Rauch SL, Shin LM, Phelps EA. Neurocircuitry models of posttraumatic stress disorder and extinction: human neuroimaging research - Past, present, and future. *Biological psychiatry*. 2006;60:376-82.

[148] True WR, Rice J, Eisen SA, Heath AC, Goldberg J, Lyons MJ, et al. A twin study of genetic and environmental contributions to liability for posttraumatic stress symptoms. *Archives of general psychiatry*. 1993 Apr;50(4):257-64.

[149] Xian H, Chantarujikapong SI, Scherrer JF, Eisen SA, Lyons MJ, Goldberg J, et al. Genetic and environmental influences on posttraumatic stress disorder, alcohol and drug dependence in twin pairs. *Drug and alcohol dependence*. 2000 Dec 22;61(1):95-102.

[150] Stein MB, Jang KL, Taylor S, Vernon PA, Livesley WJ. Genetic and environmental influences on trauma exposure and post-traumatic stress disorder symptoms: a twin study. *The American journal of psychiatry*. 2002;159(10):1675-81.

[151] Gilbertson MW, Shenton ME, Ciszewski A, Kasai K, Lasko NB, Orr SP, et al. Smaller hippocampal volume predicts pathological vulnerability to psychological trauma. *Nature neuroscience*. 2002;5(11):1242-7.

[152] Kasai K, Yamasue H, Gilbertson MW, Shenton ME, Rauch SL, Pitman RK. Evidence for acquired pregenual anterior cingulate gray matter loss from a twin study of combat-related posttraumatic stress disorder. *Biological psychiatry*. 2008 Mar 15;63(6):550-6.

[153] Davis LL, Clark DM, Kramer GL, Moeller FG, Petty F. D-fenfluramine challenge in posttraumatic stress disorder. *Biological psychiatry*. 1999 Apr 1;45(7):928-30.

[154] Southwick SM, Bremner D, Krystal JH, Charney DS. Psychobiologic research in post-traumatic stress disorder. *The Psychiatric clinics of North America*. 1994;17:251-64.

[155] Jacobs BL. Serotonin and behavior: emphasis on motor control. *The Journal of clinical psychiatry.* 1991 Dec;52 Suppl:17-23.

[156] Fichtner CG, Arora RC, O'Connor FL, Crayton JW. Platelet paroxetine binding and fluoxetine pharmacotherapy in posttraumatic stress disorder: preliminary observations on a possible predictor of clinical treatment response. *Life sciences*. 1994;54(3):PL39-44.

[157] Brady KT, Killeen TK, Brewerton T, Lucerini S. Comorbidity of psychiatric disorders and posttraumatic stress disorder. *The Journal of clinical psychiatry*. 2000;61 Suppl 7:22-32.

[158] Caspi A, Sugden K, Moffitt TE, Taylor A, Craig IW, Harrington H, et al. Influence of life stress on depression: moderation by a polymorphism in the 5-HTT gene. *Science* (New York, NY. 2003 Jul 18;301(5631):386-9.

[159] Lee HJ, Lee MS, Kang RH, Kim H, Kim SD, Kee BS, et al. Influence of the serotonin transporter promoter gene polymorphism on susceptibility to posttraumatic stress disorder. *Depression and anxiety.* 2005;21(3):135-9.

[160] Stein MB, Schork NJ, Gelernter J. Gene-by-environment (serotonin transporter and childhood maltreatment) interaction for anxiety sensitivity, an intermediate phenotype for anxiety disorders. *Neuropsychopharmacology*. 2008 Jan;33(2):312-9.

[161] Bernstein A, Zvolensky MJ. Anxiety sensitivity: selective review of promising research and future directions. *Expert review of neurotherapeutics*. 2007 Feb;7(2):97-101.

[162] Bernstein A, Zvolensky MJ, Feldner MT, Lewis SF, Fauber AL, Leen-Feldner EW, et al. Anxiety sensitivity taxon and trauma: discriminant associations for posttraumatic stress and panic symptomatology among young adults. *Depression and anxiety*. 2005;22(3):138-49.

[163] Lang AJ, Kennedy CM, Stein MB. Anxiety sensitivity and PTSD among female victims of intimate partner violence. *Depression and anxiety*. 2002;16(2):77-83.

[164] Hubler TR, Scammell JG. Intronic hormone response elements mediate regulation of FKBP5 by progestins and glucocorticoids. *Cell stress & chaperones*. 2004 Autumn;9(3):243-52.

[165] Kirchheiner J, Lorch R, Lebedeva E, Seeringer A, Roots I, Sasse J, et al. Genetic variants in FKBP5 affecting response to antidepressant drug treatment. *Pharmacogenomics*. 2008 Jul;9(7):841-6.

[166] Schiene-Fischer C, Yu C. Receptor accessory folding helper enzymes: the functional role of peptidyl prolyl cis/trans isomerases. *FEBS Letters*. 2001 Apr 20;495(1-2):1-6.

[167] Davies TH, Ning YM, Sanchez ER. A new first step in activation of steroid receptors: hormone-induced switching of FKBP51 and FKBP52 immunophilins. The *Journal of biological chemistry*. 2002 Feb 15;277(7):4597-600.

[168] Binder EB, Bradley RG, Liu W, Epstein MP, Deveau TC, Mercer KB, et al. Association of FKBP5 polymorphisms and childhood abuse with risk of posttraumatic stress disorder symptoms in adults. *Journal of the American Medical Association*. 2008 Mar 19;299(11):1291-305.

[169] Glover DA, Powers MB, Bergman L, Smits JA, Telch MJ, Stuber M. Urinary dopamine and turn bias in traumatized women with and without PTSD symptoms. *Behavioural brain research*. 2003 Sep 15;144(1-2):137-41.

[170] Hamer D. Genetics. Rethinking behavior genetics. *Science* (New York, NY. 2002 Oct 4;298(5591):71-2.

[171] Southwick SM, Paige S, Morgan CA, 3rd, Bremner JD, Krystal JH, Charney DS. Neurotransmitter alterations in PTSD: catecholamines and serotonin. *Seminars in clinical neuropsychiatry*. 1999 Oct;4(4):242-8.

[172] Bloom FE. In: Cooper JR, Bloom FE, Roth RH, eds. *The Biochemical Basis of Neuropharmacology*. New York: Oxford University Press 1982:335-46.

[173] Mustapic M, Pivac N, Kozaric-Kovacic D, Dezeljin M, Cubells JF, Muck-Seler D. Dopamine beta-hydroxylase (DBH) activity and -1021C/T polymorphism of DBH gene in combat-related post-traumatic stress disorder. *American journal of medical genetics part B, neuropsychiatric genetics*. 2007 Dec 5;144B(8):1087-9.

[174] Zabetian CP, Anderson GM, Buxbaum SG, Elston RC, Ichinose H, Nagatsu T, et al. A quantitative-trait analysis of human plasma-dopamine beta-hydroxylase activity: evidence for a major functional polymorphism at the DBH locus. *American journal of human genetics*. 2001 Feb;68(2):515-22.

[175] Cubells JF, Zabetian CP. Human genetics of plasma dopamine beta-hydroxylase activity: applications to research in psychiatry and neurology. *Psychopharmacology*. 2004 Aug;174(4):463-76.

[176] Shalev AY, Segman RH. Commentary: biological findings in PTSD -- too much or too little? *Progress in brain research*. 2008;167:187-99.

[177] Connor KM, Zhang W. Resilience: Determinants, measurement, and treatment. . *CNS Spectrums*. 2006;11(10 (Suppl 12)):5-12.

[178] McEwen BS, Stellar E. Stress and the individual. Mechanisms leading to disease. *Archives of internal medicine*. 1993 Sep 27;153(18):2093-101.

[179] Tschann JM, Kaiser P, Chesney MA, Alkon A, Boyce WT. Resilience and vulnerability among preschool children: family functioning, temperament, and behavior problems. *Journal of the American Academy of child and adolescent psychiatry*. 1996 Feb;35(2):184-92.

[180] Lesch KP, Mossner R. Genetically driven variation in serotonin uptake: is there a link to affective spectrum, neurodevelopmental, and neurodegenerative disorders? *Biological psychiatry*. 1998 Aug 1;44(3):179-92.

[181] Hariri AR, Mattay VS, Tessitore A, Kolachana B, Fera F, Goldman D, et al. Serotonin transporter genetic variation and the response of the human amygdala. *Science* (New York, NY. 2002 Jul 19;297(5580):400-3.

[182] Davidson JR, Payne VM, Connor KM, Foa EB, Rothbaum BO, Hertzberg MA, et al. Trauma, resilience and saliostasis: effects of treatment in post-traumatic stress disorder. *International clinical psychopharmacology*. 2005 Jan;20(1):43-8.

[183] Dilsaver SC, Akiskal HS, Akiskal KK, Benazzi F. Dose-response relationship between number of comorbid anxiety disorders in adolescent bipolar/unipolar disorders, and psychosis, suicidality, substance abuse and familiality. *Journal of affective disorders*. 2006 Dec;96(3):249-58.

[184] Breslau N, Davis GC, Andreski P, Federman B, Anthony JC. Epidemiological findings on posttraumatic stress disorder and comorbid disorders in the general population. *Adversity, stress, and psychopathology*. London: University Press 1998:319-28.

[185] Breslau N, Davis GC, Peterson EL, Schultz LR. A second look at comorbidity in victims of trauma: the posttraumatic stress disorder-major depression connection. *Biological psychiatry*. 2000 Nov 1;48(9):902-9.

[186] Yehuda R, LeDoux J. Response variation following trauma: a translational neuroscience approach to understanding PTSD. *Neuron*. 2007 October 4, 2007;56:19-32.

[187] Wu RS, Panusz HT, Hatch CL, Bonner WM. Histones and their modifications. *CRC Critical Reviews in Biochemistry*. 1986;20:201-63.

[188] Sutherland JE, Costa M. Epigenetics and the environment. *Annals of the New York Academy of sciences*. 2003 Mar;983:151-60.

[189] Francis DD, Champagne FA, Liu D, Meaney MJ. Maternal care, gene expression, and the development of individual differences in stress reactivity. *Annals of the New York Academy of sciences*. 1999;896:66-84.

[190] Weaver IC, Cervoni N, Champagne FA, D'Alessio AC, Sharma S, Seckl JR, et al. Epigenetic programming by maternal behavior. *Nature neuroscience*. 2004 Aug;7(8):847-54.
[191] Yehuda R, Bell A, Bierer LM, Schmeidler J. Maternal, not paternal, PTSD is related to increased risk for PTSD in offspring of Holocaust survivors. *Journal of psychiatric research*. 2008 Oct;42(13):1104-11.
[192] Wood DP, Murphy J, Center K, McLay R, Reeves D, Pyne J, et al. Combat-related post-traumatic stress disorder: a case report using virtual reality exposure therapy with physiological monitoring. *Cyberpsychology & behavior*. 2007 Apr;10(2):309-15.

INDEX

A

B

C

D

E

F

G

H

I

K

L

M

N

O

P

Q

R

S

T

U

V

W

Y